The Monnity Miracle

It's Amazing What Can Happen When You Believe.

Dr. Tyra C. Monnity

The Monnity Miracle

It's Amazing What Can Happen When You Believe

Written By: Dr. Tyra C. Monnity
Cover Designed By: Dr. Tyra C. Monnity, Aaron C. Butler
Photographs By: Dr. Tyra C. Monnity
Edited By: Aaron C. Butler

ISBN: 9781967082155 (Paperback)
ISBN: 9781967082162 (eBook)
Library of Congress Control Number: 2025905098

Printed in the United States of America

BookButler Publishing Company
Upper Marlboro, MD 20774

TheBookButler.com

BookButler Publishing Company titles may be purchased in bulk for educational, business, fundraising, or sales promotional use. For information, please email: info@thebookbutler.com

Dedication

Dedicated to those who are facing trials and tribulations that require a level of faith that allows your miracles to come to pass.

Keep praying, keep believing, keep trusting, keep advocating, and always remember it's not what man says that matters; it's what God says that matters.

Doctors treat, but God heals.

Acknowledgments

First, I offer all honor and praise to God, the savior of my life. Without you, God, none of this could happen, for without you, I am nothing. I offer you respect and admiration because it was you who provided me with the strength to create this book. It was you who provided me with the perfect words to share this story. I appreciate you being by my side every day of my life. By your power, we were granted a miracle. Thank you for being true to your word, for your faithfulness, peace, protection, support, but most of all, your love. I am honored to be a child of the most-high God.

To Aaron Butler, I sincerely appreciate you for providing me with this amazing opportunity to share my story. Your assistance, time, and knowledge are extremely valuable. You are an incredible visionary, intelligent businessperson, and entrepreneur. I appreciate you establishing a platform for black authors to be visible, acknowledged, and celebrated. A million thanks to you and your team for making sure my book(s) are published with the utmost quality. I appreciate you for turning my aspirations of being an author into a reality. It is a privilege and an honor to call you, my friend.

To my family and friends who supported us through this difficult time in our lives, "THANKS-A-MILLION." You can never truly understand the significance of your prayers, text messages, phone calls, visits, and love. We love you more than words can say. A special thank you to my mom and dad who were there for me when I really needed them most. I love you both, dearly. To my brother Dr. Quest Delaney, I appreciate your encouragement and support.

There's nothing quite like having a big brother who is always there for you. You are the greatest, and I love you 4Sure.

We extend our heartfelt thanks to the EMT's and all the doctors, nurses, specialists, and physical, occupational, and speech therapists at Holy Cross Hospital and Laurel Regional Hospital & Rehabilitation who were involved in our case for your expertise, support, and patience. You don't ever need to question whether your actions are impactful, as they truly are. We will always remember what you did for us and be eternally grateful.

To Dr. Ravinder Rustagi, you are an excellent cardiologist. I appreciate your support during this difficult time. You were accessible to me around the clock. I appreciate your guidance, attentiveness to my concerns, responses to my questions, and your support for us. You began as our cardiologist, but now you've become part of the family. We are forever grateful.

To one of the greatest pastors in the world, my pastor, John K. Jenkins, of the First Baptist Church of Glenarden International. I cannot thank you enough for being such an amazing shepherd in my life. Through your teachings on Sunday morning and Tuesday night bible study you have equipped me with the word of God. With this knowledge, I am able to stand strong against anything that does not align with God's word. You have demonstrated how "powerful prayer" is and that prayer is a tool to communicate with God. Thank you for being a shepherd who stands on the word, believes in the word, lives by the word, teaches the word and loves the word. Thank you for being a phenomenal example of what true leadership looks like and how it should operate. It is an honor and privilege to sit under your leadership, sir. I am and forever will be a dynamic disciple who will impact the world on behalf of the Lord.

To Pastors DeeKee and Briscoe, words cannot fully convey my gratitude for all that you have done for us. We appreciate your prayers and support as we navigated through this critical time in our lives. Your warrior spirits, unwavering faith, love, and encouragement helped us stand firm on God's word to receive our miracle.

Thank you to everyone who purchased my book across all platforms! Your support means the world to me, and I am so incredibly grateful for your interest in my work. THANKS-A-MILLION for helping me make my dream a reality. I love you 4Sure!

Let Me Encourage You

Trust God every day for everything.
Miracles do happen.
Nothing is impossible when you
believe and don't doubt.

Table of Content

Table of Contents

How We Met

Robert and I first met in 2007 at Howard University School of Divinity. He was working in my boss's office, fixing the light fixtures in the ceiling. When I walked in, he was standing on a ladder.

"Hello," I said, "My name is Ms. Gallman." (This was my name before we got married.)

He glanced down and smiled, "Hello, my name is Robert."

I told him that when he finished his work, he should stop by my office so I could lock up and head home. About an hour later, Robert showed up.

"Ms. Gallman, I'm finished for the day. You can lock up now," he said.

"Thank you, Robert, for letting me know," I replied.

But instead of leaving, Robert lingered. What was supposed to be a brief conversation stretched into two hours. That one moment sparked a friendship that lasted seven years—one that eventually grew into something much deeper.

Through the years, we faced our share of ups and downs, both individually and together. But no matter what, we always found our way back to each other. We loved each other enough to fight for our relationship, and as time passed, it became clear that we were meant to be more than friends.

The Monnity Miracle

When we decided to get married, we made a pact—we would be partners in everything. That meant paying for our wedding ourselves so we could have exactly what we wanted.

On August 9, 2014, we became husband and wife. Our wedding colors were pink and white, and the ceremony was short, sweet, and beautiful. Surrounded by family and friends who loved and supported us, I felt like the luckiest woman in the world.

Standing at the altar, looking into Robert's eyes, I couldn't help but reflect on everything we had gone through to get to this moment. I knew then, as I know now, that having God at the center of our relationship would be the key to sustaining our love—through the good, the bad, the happy, and the heartbreaking.

Just a year and a half into our marriage, on June 13, 2016, Robert suffered a massive stroke. It was a devastating blow, especially since he had already endured two mini-strokes in 2015 and early 2016.

That day changed both of our lives forever.

The Unexpected Call

On Monday, June 13, 2016, Robert called me at work around 12:30 p.m. He was on his way to a music store to help a friend purchase equipment for his church.

"How are you feeling?" I asked.

"Good," he replied, "The only thing I've had to drink today is a bottle of iced tea, but we're planning to grab lunch after we leave the store."

"Okay," I said, "I'll talk to you later. I love you."

"I love you too."

It was a normal conversation. Nothing seemed out of the ordinary. But three hours later, my phone rang again—this time, it wasn't Robert. It was his friend.

"Tyra, Robert just had a heart attack in the music store," he said urgently, "The paramedics are working on him now. They're taking him to the hospital."

The words hit me like a punch to the chest.

"I'm on my way," I said, my voice shaking.

I jumped up from my desk and ran full speed to my boss's office. "I have to go—my husband had a heart attack!" I barely heard her response before sprinting down the hallway, out of the building, and toward the parking garage. My hands fumbled for my keys as

The Monnity Miracle

I threw myself into the driver's seat and sped out, tires screeching against the pavement.

Holy Cross Hospital was 30 to 40 minutes away. Every second felt like an eternity. Through my tears, I prayed.

"Lord, please let him be okay."

We had only been married a year and a half. This couldn't be happening.

A Promise in the Storm

Desperate for strength, I called my mentor of over 30 years. The moment she answered, I broke down, telling her everything. She didn't hesitate—she started praying immediately.

As she prayed, I heard a still, small voice deep within me:

"He will live and not die. No matter what you see, don't agree with it or believe it. Stay focused on what I promised you. He will live and not die."

A wave of peace settled over me. I held onto those words as tightly as I could.

Once I hung up, I called my mother. I could barely get the words out.

"Mama, Robert had a heart attack. They're taking him to the hospital."

The Monnity Miracle

"Don't worry, Tyra," she said, her voice steady, "I'll meet you there. Everything is going to be okay."

I wanted to believe that.

The Hardest Call

As I sped down the highway, my mind raced. Lord, he has to be okay.

> I thought about everything we hadn't done yet—
> The trips we hadn't taken—Jamaica, California, Hawaii, the
> Bahamas, New York City, New Mexico, and Israel.
> The memories we hadn't made.
> The future we were just beginning to build.

Everything felt like it was slipping away.

Then, reality hit me—I needed to call his mother.

It was the hardest phone call I've ever had to make. How do you tell a mother that her child—her son—is fighting for his life?

My heart pounded as I dialed. When she answered, I struggled to find the right words. I told her as much as I knew, trying to hold myself together, but there was no way to soften the blow.

Hearing the heartbreak in her voice was gut-wrenching. I knew exactly how she felt. When someone you love—especially your child—is facing a life-threatening crisis, the pain is indescribable.

I hung up and gripped the steering wheel tighter. **God, I need You now more than ever.**

The Monnity Miracle

The hospital was still miles away. I pressed the gas, whispering the promise over and over again—

He will live and not die.

The Crisis Unfolds

"Robert had a heart attack."

The words didn't make sense. Just yesterday, we were sitting in the doctor's office, making plans for the future. How had we gone from that to this? My heart pounded as my mind scrambled to grasp the reality crashing down on me.

The words slammed into me, knocking the breath from my lungs. "What?" I whispered, gripping the phone as if I could steady myself against the weight of what I was hearing.

And then, in the background, I heard it—chaos. Shouting voices. The sharp commands of emergency responders. A machine beeping erratically. And then—dear God—the sound of paddles charging, followed by a deafening shock.

"No pulse! Charging again—clear!"

Another surge of electricity. Another desperate attempt to bring my husband back.

I don't remember grabbing my keys. I don't remember running to my car. All I knew was that I had to get to Robert. Had to see him. Had to know if he was still alive.

The drive was a blur—lights flashing past, my fingers clenched around the steering wheel, my breath coming in short, panicked gasps. Every red light was an enemy, every slow-moving car an unbearable obstacle. I gripped the wheel tighter, whispering over and over, "Please, God. Please."

The Chaos

When I finally reached the hospital, I rushed to the information desk.

"Where is my husband?"

The nurse looked up at me with an expression of indifference. "What is your husband's name?"

"Robert Monnity. I was told he was brought in a few minutes ago."

She shuffled through stacks of paperwork, glanced at the patient monitor, and then looked back at me, "I don't see his name here."

Panic surged through me, "That can't be right! I just spoke with someone from this hospital who confirmed he was here."

I silently prayed, "Lord, please help me not to say the wrong thing."

Just then, I spotted Robert's friend, Pastor DeeKee. He embraced me, his face full of sorrow. "I'm so sorry," he murmured.

Before I could respond, the nurse interrupted, "I'll check in the back," disappearing behind the double doors.

I turned and scanned the waiting area. The emergency room was a scene of absolute chaos. Every seat was occupied, and people stood against the walls, shifting impatiently as they waited their turn. Small children climbed on the furniture, their laughter and shrieks cutting through the tension in the room. Patients clutched clipboards, hurriedly filling out medical forms, while others argued with staff about the long wait times. Groans of pain echoed from different corners, a stark reminder of the suffering surrounding me.

But I barely registered any of it. My mind had one singular focus—getting to Robert.

The nurse returned, "Yes, your husband is here. Follow me."

I immediately got up and followed her through the double doors. As we walked, a doctor stepped into the hallway, her expression unreadable.

"Mrs. Monnity?"

"Yes?"

"Your husband flatlined five times during the ambulance ride. He has been intubated and is currently on life support. He is legally brain dead."

She never even looked up from his chart.

I repeated her words, my voice barely above a whisper, "Legally brain dead?"

She nodded, her tone cold and detached.

Then she asked, "Mrs. Monnity, what do you want us to do?"

Stepping into Advocacy and Faith

"Take me to my husband."

She led me to the registration desk, where they took my picture and driver's license. A visitor's badge was handed to me, and I was instructed to follow her.

As I stepped into the elevator, I heard that still, small voice:

"He will live and not die. Whatever you do, do not agree with what you see."

When I entered Robert's ICU room at 7:25 p.m., an unexplainable peace settled over me. But as I looked at him, the sight stole the breath from my lungs.

He lay motionless, tubes snaking in and out of his body, machines beeping softly around him. My hands trembled, and my chest tightened, but I swallowed the tears burning behind my eyes. There was no room for weakness. I had to be strong. I had to be present, even when all I wanted to do was collapse.

Dr. Duane Stillion was the first doctor to speak to me about Robert's condition. He explained in great detail that Robert did not suffer a heart attack, but an Ischemic Stroke. A blood clot blocked an artery in his brain, cutting off the flow to part of his brain. He was under heavy sedation, and the only thing keeping him alive was the ventilator.

The Monnity Miracle

"There is no brain activity," he said, "He is legally brain dead. It doesn't look good."

And then, just like that, he left the room, leaving me alone with Robert.

I sat in the chair by the window, my mind racing. I could hear the scripture in my spirit:

"To be absent from the body is to be present with the Lord." *(2 Corinthians 5:8)*

The only thing I could do was pray. "God, help me," I whispered, my fingers tightening into fists at my sides, "Please."

Another doctor entered the room. "We need to insert an A-line and C-line," he explained.

I had no idea what those were. He patiently described them—what they did, why Robert needed them. He handed me an authorization form.

"Do you have any questions?"

I shook my head, "Not right now."

After he left, Pastor DeeKee walked in. I told him everything the doctor had just said.

"I've never had to handle anything like this," I admitted, my voice shaking, "I just want to make the right decision for Robert."

The Monnity Miracle

Pastor DeeKee sat beside me. We prayed together, asking God for wisdom, for clarity. Afterward, he squeezed my hand and left.

Through the fear, the helplessness, the unbearable uncertainty, I could feel God's presence. The Holy Spirit was guiding me, step by step, even as my world crumbled.

I pulled out my laptop and started researching. I needed to know more about the A-line and C-line—what they did, the risks, the benefits. The doctor had explained, but I wanted to be sure.

After gaining a better understanding, I signed the form.

By this time, it was around 9:00 p.m. My mother, Alice, and my sister, Apria, had arrived. They were waiting for me in the lobby.

The moment I saw my mother, she wrapped me in a hug. Her warmth, her presence—it was everything I needed.

There's something about seeing your mother when you're facing a storm. Mothers have a way of making you feel like you can get through anything.

They stayed with me overnight, offering comfort, support, and—thankfully—food. I hadn't eaten all day.

After forcing down a few bites, I tried to sleep. But every time I closed my eyes, I saw Robert hooked up to all those machines.

I kept repeating the promise God whispered to me:

"He will live and not die. He will live and not die. He will live and not die."

The Monnity Miracle

At that moment, I realized just how quickly life can change. One moment, you're walking and talking without a care in the world. The next, you're fighting for your life.

I thought about everything I had learned in church—about faith, trust, and believing in God.

A verse from Hebrews came to mind:

"But without faith it is impossible to please Him: for he that cometh to God must believe that He is, and that He is a rewarder of them that diligently seek Him." *(Hebrews 11:6)*

I knew then that my faith had to be unshakable. There was no room for doubt. I had to stand on His promise.

I had to believe.

I didn't know what the next minute, the next hour, the next day would bring. But I knew one thing with absolute certainty—Robert was not alone. And neither was I.

God's Promise

"For we walk by faith, not by sight."

2 Corinthians 5:7

In life, you will not always be able to see what has been promised to you today. You have to have faith that it is coming even though you haven't seen it yet.

The Power of Prayer

At exactly 6:00 a.m., I woke up, splashed cold water on my face, brushed my teeth, fixed my hair, and applied just enough makeup to mask the exhaustion pressing behind my eyes. As I stared at my reflection in the mirror, the weight of it all settled over me—I had barely closed my eyes, yet the night had felt like a lifetime. The events of the previous day replayed in my mind—Robert's unresponsive, the doctors' grim expressions, the tubes keeping him alive. Every detail was seared into my memory, yet I refused to accept that this was the end.

Robert needed me to be strong.

I took a shaky breath and reached for my phone. My fingers scrolled automatically to the healing scriptures I had bookmarked the night before. My mind was racing, but I knew one thing for certain—if I was going to get through this, I needed to stay anchored in the Word.

The doctors would be making their rounds soon, and I needed to be at Robert's side. I needed to remind myself—and him—that God had the final say.

I sat in the chair beside his bed. The room smelled of antiseptic and medical equipment, the rhythmic beeping of the monitors breaking the heavy silence. Sunlight filtered through the window, casting a glow over Robert's still form. I took Robert's hand in mine and began speaking life over him. I wasn't just reading scriptures; I was declaring war against the spirit of death that had tried to take him.

The Monnity Miracle

- *"Fear not, for I am with you; be not dismayed, for I am your God. I will strengthen you, yes, I will help you, I will uphold you with my righteous right hand."* — Isaiah 41:10
- *"LORD my God, I called to you for help, and you healed me."* — Psalm 30:2
- *"The Lord sustains them on their sickbed and restores them from their bed of illness."* — Psalm 41:3
- *"Heal me, O LORD, and I shall be healed; save me, and I shall be saved, for you are my praise."* — Jeremiah 17:14

With every word, I willed my spirit to believe.

"Robert, you are healed in Jesus' name," I whispered, "You will live and not die."

I refused to allow any space for doubt because I knew doubt could weaken my faith. And if my faith wavered, if I allowed even an inch of disbelief to creep in, I feared it would be an opening for the enemy to win.

Robert was going to live. He *had* to live.

The door opened, and the doctors entered. They seemed surprised to see me sitting at Robert's bedside.

"Good morning, Mrs. Monnity. We are here to take a look at Robert."

They nodded at me before stepping toward Robert's bed. The examination was routine, but to me, it was everything.

The Monnity Miracle

One of the doctors leaned over, pried open Robert's eyes, and shined a flashlight into them. First, the right eye. Nothing. Then the left. Still nothing.

I held my breath, waiting. Hoping.

The doctor turned to me, his voice as clinical as ever, "I'm sorry, Mrs. Monnity, there has been no change."

I exhaled, but I didn't falter. My faith would not be shaken.

"That's okay," I said, my voice unwavering, "He will be fine."

Collective Prayer and Strengthening Faith

The doctor studied me for a moment. "Has anyone explained the severity of his condition to you?"

I smiled, calm and steady, "Yes, they have."

He didn't say anything else. Instead, he gave me a small nod and walked out with his team.

As the door shut behind them, I leaned over Robert's bed, my lips close to his ear. *It doesn't matter what they say; the power belongs to God.*

I pulled out my phone, searched YouTube, and played Hezekiah Walker's *Power Belongs to God.* The words of the song filled the room, wrapping around us like armor.

There is nothing too hard for God.

The Monnity Miracle

I closed my eyes and let the music settle into my spirit.

Pastor Jenkins has always taught us about the power of collective prayer. Matthew 18:19-20 says, *"Again I say to you that if two of you agree on earth concerning anything that they ask, it will be done for them by My Father in heaven. For where two or three are gathered together in My name, I am there in the midst of them."*

I sent out the first of what would become daily messages:

"Please continue to pray for Robert. The doctors say there's no change, but we know that God has the final say. I'm standing on His promises, and I ask that you do the same."

The messages poured in, each one a lifeline. I wasn't standing alone. An army of believers was standing with me. I felt their prayers.

Advocacy: The Importance of Being Present

As prayers continued to pour in, I knew that faith alone wasn't enough—I also had to be vigilant. Trusting God didn't mean being passive; it meant standing guard over Robert in every possible way.

Doctors, nurses, and specialists rotated in and out of his room all day. I learned their names, departments, and roles in Robert's care. I took notes on everything—every medication, every test result, every recommendation. If they were going to do something to my husband, I was going to know about it.

I wasn't just Robert's wife at this moment. I was his advocate.

The Monnity Miracle

A year earlier, Robert had suffered a mini-stroke, and I had learned something critical—hospitals run differently when someone is watching. When no one is there to advocate for a patient, things fall through the cracks. Decisions get made without consultation. I refused to let that happen to Robert.

I also prayed for the doctors, the nurses, the techs. Because I knew they weren't just dealing with Robert—they were carrying the weight of every patient under their care. They had good days and bad days. They are human, and humans make mistakes.

So, I prayed. I prayed for their wisdom, their focus, and their compassion. I prayed that God would guide their hands and their decisions.

As the evening approached, exhaustion started to pull at me, but I refused to leave. I looked over at Robert's motionless body; the beeping monitors a steady rhythm in the background.

There were no signs of progress yet. No movement. No response.

But I kept trusting.

I didn't know what tomorrow would bring.

But I knew this—prayer was my weapon, and I was going to use it.

God's Promise

Trust in the LORD with all thine heart; and lean not unto thine own understanding. In all your ways acknowledge Him,

And He shall direct your paths.
Proverbs 3:5,6

We need to realize that we don't know everything, but we have a God who does. Sometimes, when we think we are doing the right thing, it may not be the right thing. If you go to God and ask Him to help you with your situation, He will give you a plan to get through it.

The Long Nights

Nights in the ICU were relentless. I quickly learned there would be no distinction between one day and the next—just an endless stretch of beeping machines, hushed conversations in the hall, and the steady sound of Robert's ventilator. Sleep was a distant luxury. I refused to leave his side for long, afraid that if I did, something might happen.

I got as comfortable as I could in the chair beside his bed, my body aching from exhaustion. I would doze off for minutes at a time, never fully resting, always snapping awake at the sound of footsteps approaching the room. Every time a nurse or doctor entered, I would be alert, making sure I knew exactly what they were doing, what medications they were administering, and what changes, if any, were happening in Robert's condition.

The weight of it all pressed down on me—physically, mentally, emotionally. The longer I sat in that room, the heavier it became. I knew I needed to be strong, but strength was starting to feel like a battle.

At 2:30 a.m., I made the difficult decision to leave for a short while. I needed a shower. I needed fresh clothes. But more than anything, I needed a moment to release the pressure that had been building inside me. I asked one of the hospital staff to sit with Robert until I returned.

The house was eerily silent when I stepped inside, a stark contrast to the chaos of the hospital. As soon as I turned on the shower, the reality of everything hit me all at once. The water washed over me, and before I could stop myself, I broke.

The Monnity Miracle

I sobbed like a child, my body trembling under the weight of everything I had been holding in. I let the tears come, knowing that for a brief moment, I didn't have to be strong. I didn't have to hold it all together.

But even in my breakdown, I knew I couldn't stay there.

"God, I need You," I whispered through my tears, "I can't do this without You."

When the tears finally slowed, I took a deep breath and stepped out of the shower. I changed into fresh clothes, gathered what I needed, and headed back to the hospital.

Advocacy: Doing the Research

The moment I walked back into Robert's room, I felt the weight settle onto my shoulders again, but this time, I knew I wasn't carrying it alone.

I again got as comfortable as I could in the chair, dozing in and out of sleep.

By 6:00 a.m., I was awake again, methodically following the same steps as the day before. The monotony of washing my face and brushing my teeth gave me a fleeting sense of normalcy. Once dressed, I moved quickly back to Robert's room. The hum of machines greeted me, as did the stillness of his form. I took his hand and began reading verses aloud, letting their rhythm fill the quiet air. Robert's condition hadn't changed, but I refused to let doubt take root. I wouldn't allow even the smallest crack for fear to creep in. No matter how bleak the prognosis seemed, I held tightly to the promise that this routine would not be wasted. I believed these small acts mattered.

When the doctors arrived for their morning rounds, they looked surprised to see me still there. They had been through this routine before—check Robert's vitals, shine a light into his eyes, report no change. But what they didn't understand was that I would be here every single day, watching, questioning, and ensuring Robert received the best possible care.

"Good morning, Mrs. Monnity," one of them said, "We're here to take a look at Robert."

I nodded, sitting upright, ready to take in every word.

One of the doctors took out his flashlight and leaned over Robert's bed, prying open his eyes one at a time. He shined the light into the right eye—nothing. Then the left—still nothing.

"Sorry, Mrs. Monnity," he said with practiced sympathy, "There has been no change."

I met his gaze, unwavering. "That's okay. He will be fine. God's got him."

They exchanged glances but didn't argue.

Before they left, I made a request, "I'd like a copy of his medication list, please."

A nurse brought it to me about fifteen minutes later. As I scanned the list, three medications stood out—Fentanyl, Zofran, and Propofol. I pulled out my laptop and started researching, determined to understand their effects and potential risks. If the doctors were giving Robert something, I needed to know exactly what it was doing to his body.

While researching, I made sure Robert knew I was still present.

"You are not alone," I whispered, "I am here. I'm fighting for you on this side, so I need you to fight on that side. You can't leave me now. We are just starting our lives together."

I studied his face, searching for any sign that he could hear me. A twitch. A flicker. Anything.

But there was nothing.

And yet, deep in my spirit, I felt something shift.

Just out of the corner of my eye, I saw him—Robert's Spirit Man, standing near the chair in the room. I gasped, my heart pounding. He was there. He was still here.

I squeezed his hand tightly. "I know you hear me," I whispered.

The Spiritual Battle and Renewed Commitment

A new determination settled over me.

I wasn't going anywhere.

At some point, I realized that if I was going to fight for Robert, I needed to take care of myself, too.

The Monnity Miracle

Even when I wasn't hungry, I made myself eat. I walked down to the hospital cafeteria, using the time away from the machines to gather my thoughts and refocus my mind. It was easier to meditate on God's word outside of the ICU, away from the constant beeping and medical discussions.

Every night, I sat in that silent room, listening. Hoping. Waiting for God to tell me what to do next.

I talked to Him about everything—about my fears, about Robert's doctors, about the decisions I had to make. I prayed for the nurses, the specialists, and everyone who had a hand in Robert's care. I prayed for wisdom, for strength, for clarity.

And in those moments, peace was there. It had always been there.

As exhaustion crept in again, I reclined in the chair and let my thoughts drift to the day Robert and I exchanged vows.

"I, Tyra, take you, Robert, to be my husband, to have and to hold from this day forward, for better or for worse, for richer, for poorer, in sickness and in health...to love and to cherish, from this day forward, until death do us part."

This was what that promise meant. Not just the good days, the easy days—but the hard ones. The ones that tested every fiber of my being.

Even if he couldn't see me or hear me, I was going to love him through this.

The Monnity Miracle

It was around 11:00 pm when I settled deeper into my chair, gripping his hand once more. "You will live and not die," I whispered.

I didn't know how long this fight would last.

But I knew this—I wasn't giving up.

Not now.

Not ever.

God's Promise

May the God of hope fill you with all joy and peace as you trust in him, so that you may overflow with hope by the power of the Holy Spirit.

Romans 15:13

When you are facing difficult situations, it's hard to find joy in them, but if you trust in God, He will give you peace that surpasses all understanding through the power of the Holy Spirit. Making you feel hopeful in the situation.

A Quiet Resolve

The mornings were now a ritual. My eyes carried the weight of sleepless nights, but this new routine somehow grounded me, giving me a small semblance of control in a life that felt anything but steady. Each stroke of the brush against my hair, each splash of water on my face, was a moment to prepare my mind for the hours ahead. Exhaustion clung to me, but I refused to let it take over. Robert needed me alert, present, and unwavering.

By the time I reached his bedside, I was ready to fight again. I gripped his hand and whispered the same declarations I had spoken the day before and the day before that. I wasn't just reading scripture—I was speaking life into his body, calling him back in the name of Jesus.

- *"Fear not, for I am with you; be not dismayed, for I am your God. I will strengthen you, yes, I will help you, I will uphold you with my righteous right hand." — Isaiah 41:10*
- *"LORD my God, I called to you for help, and you healed me." — Psalm 30:2*
- *"The Lord sustains them on their sickbed and restores them from their bed of illness." — Psalm 41:3*
- *"Heal me, O LORD, and I shall be healed; save me, and I shall be saved, for you are my praise." — Jeremiah 17:14*

When the doctors arrived for their morning rounds, I remained seated, steady, and unshaken. They came with the same report, expecting me to accept their words as final.

"Good morning, Mrs. Monnity," one of them said, "We're here to check on Robert."

I simply nodded.

One of the doctors leaned over, pried open Robert's eyes, and shined the flashlight into them. First, the right. Nothing. Then the left. Still nothing.

The doctor sighed and looked at me, "I'm sorry, Mrs. Monnity, but there is still no change."

I met his gaze without hesitation, "That's okay. He will be fine. God has it all in control."

I could see the confusion in his eyes. Maybe he expected me to break down, to finally accept their prognosis. But he didn't understand—I had received my report from God long before I walked into that hospital, and I was standing on His word.

Advocacy: Being His Voice

After the doctors left, I shifted into advocacy mode. If Robert couldn't speak for himself, I would be his voice.

After sending out the morning text to family and friends with the usual update and prayer request, I checked every tube, every line—oxygen tubes, face guides, IVs, catheter, compression stockings, the A-line, the C-line—making sure nothing was out of place. Then, I requested Robert's updated medication list. When the nurse handed it to me, I pulled out my laptop and got to work. I looked up each drug, its purpose, and its side effects. I took notes, determined to ask the doctors about them later. If they were administering something that wasn't necessary or could cause complications, I needed to know.

Even as I fought for him medically, I kept my focus on the spiritual battle at hand. Throughout the day, I played gospel music in his room, hoping to stir something in his spirit.

- *Hezekiah Walker – "Power Belongs to God"*
- *Kirk Franklin – "He's Able"*
- *William Becton – "Be Encouraged"*
- *Fred Hammond – "No Weapon"*
- *VaShawn Mitchell – "Turning Around for Me"*

Even though they told me he was brain-dead, I refused to accept that as the final word. I had seen him in the spirit the day before, standing behind the chair. I knew he was still fighting, still trying to make his way back. Every song, every prayer, every word spoken in that room was preparing for the manifestation of what I already believed.

The Test of Faith and Love

Even as I monitored his care and ensured every detail was accounted for, I knew that faith and prayer had to remain just as active. I wasn't alone in believing for Robert's healing—our family, friends, and church community stood with me. Throughout the day, I spoke with them on the phone. Encouragement and prayers were sent my way. We prayed that when Robert woke up, there would be no lingering effects—no memory loss, no fatigue, no speech or mobility issues. We were believing God for a full and complete restoration.

The Monnity Miracle

As the hours stretched into the night, I stayed by Robert's side, whispering to him and holding his hand, "You are not alone. I am here. I need you to fight with me."

Memories of our life together flooded my mind—our laughter, our dreams, our plans. But one memory still held me captive—our wedding day. The vows we spoke echoed in my mind: In sickness and in health. I had never felt the weight of those words more than in this moment. This was the test of commitment, of loyalty, of love in its purest form.

Two weeks before Robert's stroke, I had been reading the story of Lazarus. I had praised God for breathing life back into Lazarus, never realizing that just days later, I would be living that same story. Now, here I was, standing in the gap, believing that the same resurrection power that raised Lazarus would raise my husband.

This was a refining process—a strengthening of faith, an unshakable trust in God's word. I knew He was with me. I felt His presence guiding me, instructing me on what to ask, what to say, and what steps to take next.

As exhaustion set in, I settled into the chair once more, gripping Robert's hand.

"You will live and not die," I whispered one last time before drifting off to sleep.

No matter how long it took, I wasn't leaving. Not until I saw the miracle I was believing for.

God's Promise

Therefore, I tell you, whatever you ask in prayer, believe that you have received it, and it will be yours.

Mark 11:24

When you go to God in prayer, whatever you are asking for, believe in your heart that you have already received it, and you will have it at the appointed time according to God's will for your life.

The Long Vigil

My steps became automatic, a well-rehearsed dance leading me back to the chair beside Robert's hospital bed. The days blurred together, but one thing remained the same—I would not stop fighting.

I no longer needed my phone to reference the healing scriptures; they were ingrained in me now, stitched into the fabric of my prayers. They were my anthem, my lifeline, my shield against the unrelenting storm of doubt and discouragement.

I spoke them softly, each word settling into the sterile hospital air like a comforting blanket.

When the doctors arrived, their presence was no longer a jolt to my system. The routine had become familiar.

"Sorry, Mrs. Monnity," the doctor said, his voice carrying the same detached sympathy I had heard for days, "We still don't see any change."

I met his gaze, steady and unwavering, "That's okay. Robert will be fine."

He hesitated for a moment before nodding, and I wondered if he was confused or frustrated by my certainty. Each day, it became clearer that they expected me to let go. But they didn't understand—I had my report from God, and I refused to accept anything less than His promise.

Strength Through Support

As I was sending out my daily text update to family and friends, my phone buzzed. It was Robert's friend, Pastor DeeKee.

"I want to come by to visit Robert. Is that okay?"

"Yes," I replied without hesitation.

An hour later, he arrived. His warm hug felt like a lifeline, grounding me for just a moment.

"How are you holding up?" he asked.

I managed a small smile, "I'm okay."

He walked over to Robert's bedside without hesitation and placed a firm hand on his arm. His voice filled the room as he prayed, his faith as strong as mine.

"Robert, I know you can hear me. In the matchless name of Jesus Christ, I command you to come forth! Just as the Lord called Lazarus back to life, I declare in the name of Jesus, you will rise again!"

His words carried authority, an unshakable belief that echoed my own. I gripped Robert's hand and silently agreed with every declaration he made.

When he finished, he looked at Robert with certainty, "I'll see you soon, my brother."

The Monnity Miracle

I walked him to the lobby, his encouragement echoing in my spirit. *Keep standing. God is moving.*

A Shift in the Atmosphere

When I stepped back into Robert's room, something had changed. The air felt different—lighter, charged with expectancy. I couldn't see it yet, but I could feel it.

I began thanking God, not just for what I hoped He would do, but for what He had already done. Instead of asking for healing, I *thanked* Him for it.

I moved to Robert's side and laid my hands on him. "Thank You, Lord, for restoring his body. Thank You for giving him life. Thank You for bringing him back to me."

For the first time, when the nurses entered, they didn't look at me with quiet pity. Instead, their expressions softened with something else—respect, maybe even admiration.

One nurse hesitated before speaking, "Mrs. Monnity, I just want to say… I really admire your dedication to your husband. Your being here every day is making a difference."

Another nurse, standing near the monitor, nodded, "Most patients don't have someone here 24/7 like this. It really does matter."

A third nurse smiled as she adjusted Robert's IV, "We see it, you know—the love, the faith. It's inspiring."

This was the first time I felt like the hospital staff wasn't gently nudging me toward letting go.

The Monnity Miracle

"Thank you," I whispered, both to them and to God.

That night, as I prepared to lay down, my spirit was so stirred that sleep felt impossible.

I thought about Robert's dreams—the ones he had whispered to me late at night. He wanted to start his own company, *iRobert Services.* He had planned to go back to school for his Bachelor's Degree in Computer Science. He wanted to travel.

None of that had happened yet.

I couldn't give up.

This wasn't just about survival. It was about everything we were still meant to do.

I lay back in the recliner, the hum of the machines filling the quiet. The monitors cast a faint glow over the room, and exhaustion finally began to pull at me. Every time I stirred, I whispered another prayer.

Morning would come soon enough.

And I would be ready to witness God working.

God's Promise

LORD my God, I called to you for help, and you healed me.
$$\text{Psalm 30:2}$$

God is always waiting and willing to heal us of any sickness or disease if we would just reach out to Him for help. He is always listening and waiting for you to call on Him.

Resurrection Power

Waking up this morning, I felt different than the previous mornings. There is an unexplainable certainty settling deep in my spirit. Pastor DeeKee's powerful prayer from the day before still echoed in my mind, and last night's petition to God left me with renewed strength.

Like clockwork, I moved through my morning routine. Each action—splashing cold water on my face, brushing my teeth, fixing my hair—was automatic, but my heart felt lighter. I made my way back to Robert's room, anticipation coursing through me. I didn't know how, and I didn't know when, but I was convinced that today was going to be different.

I sat beside Robert, taking his hand in mine. As always, I spoke the healing scriptures over him, declaring God's promises with unwavering faith.

When the doctors arrived for their rounds, I didn't flinch. They performed their usual tests—leaning over Robert, prying open each eye, shining their tiny flashlight inside. Right eye. Nothing. Left eye. Nothing.

"Sorry, Mrs. Monnity, we still don't see any change," one doctor said, his tone heavy with regret.

"It's alright."

Instead of just walking out as usual, he hesitated before adding, "I really wish we had better news for you."

The Monnity Miracle

I nodded but remained steady, "It's okay."

They left the room slowly, their faces filled with sympathy, but I refused to accept their report as final. With every breath, I trusted and believed that God would do what He had promised—to resurrect Robert.

I leaned over Robert and whispered, "They don't know the God we serve. He has the final say."

When Faith Meets Advocacy

After the doctors left, I moved through my regular routine of checking Robert's medical equipment. I examined his oxygen tubes, IV lines, catheter, and compression stockings—every detail had to be accounted for. I knew the side effects of his medications and watched for any adverse reactions. I requested his vitals from the nurse, making sure I understood everything they were monitoring.

Shortly after, a respiratory specialist came in to check Robert's breathing. I asked how Robert was doing, and he responded, "So far, so good."

Then, something unexpected happened. He paused, looked at me, and said, "You know, I've been watching you here every day. Your husband is a lucky man. A lot of people don't have anyone."

His words took me by surprise.

"When you're in a critical situation like this, you need someone to advocate for you," I told him, "Someone has to make sure you're cared for when you can't speak for yourself."

The Monnity Miracle

I thanked him for his kind words, but in my heart, I thanked God. This was another confirmation that I was exactly where I needed to be—fighting for Robert, standing in the gap, refusing to give up.

I sat back down and took out my phone. Scrolling to my favorite gospel playlist, I hit play on *Power Belongs to God* by Hezekiah Walker. The lyrics filled the room, strengthening my spirit. I let the song repeat, each time stirring up my faith even more.

Something was happening. I could feel it.

The Monnity Miracle

That afternoon, my mentors, Pastors Briscoe, arrived to visit Robert. They had been in my life for over 30 years and had always been a source of wisdom and strength. After their Sunday service, they came straight to the hospital.

When they arrived, I met them in the lobby, and they embraced me warmly. "How are you holding up?" they asked.

"I'm trusting God for a miracle," I said simply.

We walked down the hallway together, and the moment they stepped into Robert's room, the entire atmosphere shifted. The presence of God was thick in the air.

They stood at Robert's bedside and immediately went into prayer. Pastor Briscoe's voice was strong and full of authority as he called Robert forth, just as Jesus called Lazarus from the grave.

"Robert, in the name of Jesus, rise up!"

The Monnity Miracle

In my spirit, I agreed with every word. They anointed his body and the entire room with oil, declaring healing, life, and restoration. The power of God was tangible, and as they finished, we all knew—something had broken in the spirit.

We walked out of the room, confident in what had taken place. As we reached the lobby, I thanked them for coming and promised to keep them updated.

At 7:00 p.m., as I sat in my chair beside Robert's bed, I suddenly heard a quiet voice within my spirit.

Get your phone and walk over to Robert's bed.

I immediately stood, reached into my purse, and pulled out my phone, just as the Holy Spirit instructed.

Turn on your camera.

My heart pounded as I obeyed. Just as I raised my phone, at exactly 7:05 p.m., Robert's eyes opened.

Wide. Clear. Fiery red.

I gasped, frozen for a second before finding my voice.

"Robert! Robert! Robert!" I cried, gripping his hand, "How are you Sweet P?"

His head moved slightly. He nodded. He couldn't speak because of the breathing tube, but I saw the recognition in his eyes.

The Monnity Miracle

Tears flooded my face as joy exploded in my chest. "He will live and not die," I whispered through my sobs, "Glory be to God. Hallelujah! Thank You, Jesus!"

I ran to the nurse's station, barely able to contain my excitement, "He's awake! His eyes are open!"

The nurses rushed into the room, one by one, their eyes widening as they took in what was happening.

The nurse on duty immediately paged Dr. Stillion. Within minutes, word spread across the ICU. Staff members who had been working on Robert's case since the beginning stopped by, amazed and in awe of the miracle unfolding before them.

"I've never seen anything like this," one nurse murmured.

Another whispered, "This is incredible."

I turned to them and smiled, "When you trust and believe in God, amazing things happen."

The moment settled into my spirit, and I knew—I had witnessed a miracle.

I stepped outside the room to call Robert's mother. The moment she heard my voice, she knew something had happened.

"Robert's awake," I told her.

She burst into tears, praising God. I could hear the relief, the joy, the answered prayers in her cries.

The Monnity Miracle

Next, I called Pastor Briscoe. The moment they answered, I shouted, "He's awake! Robert opened his eyes!"

Tears of joy streamed down my face as we rejoiced together over the phone. "Tyra, don't thank us," Pastor Briscoe said, "Thank God. He is the one who did this."

That night, sleep eluded me. I sat in my chair, watching Robert, overwhelmed with gratitude.

"God, You are amazing," I whispered, "There is nothing too hard for You. Thank You for being a God who keeps His promises."

For the first time in days, I allowed my body to rest. I didn't know what tomorrow would bring, but I knew this—Robert was coming back to me.

God had spoken.

And He had the final say.

God's Promise

Is anyone among you sick? Let them call the elders of the church to pray over them and anoint them with oil in the name of the Lord. And the prayer offered in faith will make the sick person well; the Lord will raise them up. If they have sinned, they will be forgiven.

James 5:14-15

If you or a family member are sick, you ought to request the church elders to pray for you and to anoint you with oil. They believe that praying with faith will ultimately lead to healing. As a result, you or your family member will recover fully.

53

Power Belongs to God

A New Day, A New Beginning

I woke up the next morning with anticipation stirring in my spirit. Something was different. The weight of uncertainty that had hung over me for days was lifting. I didn't know what the day would bring, but I knew God wasn't finished yet.

As I stretched, I could hear the low murmur of conversation outside the door. When I stepped into the hallway, I was surprised to see more nurses and doctors gathered at the nurses' station than usual. Some were smiling, others exchanged hushed words, and then one turned toward me.

"Good morning, Mrs. Monnity," she said warmly, "I heard the wonderful news last night."

I nodded, a smile breaking across my face, "Yes, all glory belongs to God."

Another woman, a family member of a different patient, approached me as I walked toward the restroom. "Congratulations," she said, her voice filled with sincerity, "I heard about your husband this morning. I pray he makes a full recovery."

"In the name of Jesus, I receive that," I responded, feeling the power of those words resonate in my heart.

By the time I returned to Robert's room, the doctors had already arrived, preparing for their morning assessment.

The Evidence of a Miracle

"Good morning, sir," one of the doctors said, his voice carrying a lightness I hadn't heard before. "You really gave us and your wife quite the scare."

Robert, now slightly upright in his hospital bed, locked eyes with the doctor. He couldn't speak yet—the intubation tube still in his mouth—but he was awake. He was aware. He was present.

The doctor stepped closer, flashlight in hand, and carefully checked Robert's pupils. For the first time since he had been admitted, they responded to the light.

"All right, your eyes are a little red right now, but they will clear up soon," the doctor assured him, "Can you blink for me? Once for no, twice for yes."

Robert blinked twice.

"Is your name Robert?"

Blink. Blink.

"Do you know where you are?"

Blink. Blink.

"Is this beautiful woman sitting next to you your wife?"

Blink. Blink.

The Monnity Miracle

The doctor let out a small laugh, shaking his head in amazement, "Very good."

Next, he slid his finger into Robert's palm, "Can you squeeze my finger?"

Robert blinked twice, then slowly curled his fingers around the doctor's hand.

The room went silent.

He repeated the test with Robert's left hand and then asked if he could move his toes. Again, Robert responded.

For six days, these same doctors had examined my husband, finding no signs of life beyond what the machines provided. Now, before their very eyes, Robert was communicating, moving, responding.

One of them exhaled deeply, shaking his head. "The next step is removing the intubation tube," he said, looking at Robert, "Does that sound like a good deal to you?"

Blink. Blink.

Before leaving, the doctor turned back to Robert and said, "You are a miracle."

Sharing the Testimony

Not long after, one of the nurses who had seen Robert when he first arrived peeked into the room.

"I heard Robert was awake," he said, "I had to come see for myself."

As he stepped closer, he stopped abruptly, his hands covering his mouth. His eyes welled with tears as he stared at Robert in disbelief.

"I can't believe this is the same man I saw a few days ago."

I placed a hand over my heart, overwhelmed with gratitude. "Thank you for everything you did to help my husband," I told him, "Do you want to come closer?"

He shook his head, still in shock, but then smiled, "Thank you for letting me see him."

Later, the doctor pulled me aside to discuss Robert's next steps.

"We're going to schedule an MRI, blood work, and a chest X-ray," he explained, "We also need to review his medications. Additionally, I'll be sending the therapy team in tomorrow morning to evaluate his condition—speech, occupational, and physical therapy."

"I'll be here," I assured him.

He gave me a knowing smile, "I figured as much."

When he left, I turned to Robert and whispered, "They haven't seen anything yet."

The Monnity Miracle

The words of 1 Corinthians 2:9 echoed in my mind: *'Eye has not seen, nor ear heard, nor have entered into the heart of man the things which God has prepared for those who love Him.'*

I knew—this was just the beginning.

The Call to Advocate

That morning, as I checked Robert's lines and monitors, I realized how different it felt now that he was awake. I explained every step to him, making sure he understood what was happening. He nodded slightly, acknowledging me.

For the first time in nearly a week, I wasn't just talking *at* him—I was talking *to* him.

The nurse and respiratory therapist entered, and I quickly shifted into advocacy mode, ensuring I received Robert's updated vitals and medication list. The respiratory therapist smiled as he reviewed Robert's breathing.

"He's improving faster than I expected," he admitted, "This is a miracle—I've never seen anyone recover this quickly."

I grinned, "Glory be to God! My God is able."

The therapist chuckled, "If he keeps progressing like this, we might be able to take him off the ventilator tomorrow."

I met his eyes with certainty. "Not *if*—*when*."

Encouraging Others

As the day went on, word continued to spread. Phone calls, text messages, and even visitors flooded in—each one rejoicing in what God had done.

Other families in the ICU stopped me in the hallway, asking about Robert's story. Some were facing their own battles with loved ones in critical condition, and I could see the desperation in their eyes.

I shared my testimony and encouraged them to fight for their loved ones, just as I had for Robert.

"You are your loved one's best advocate," I told them, "Be present. Get involved. Ask questions. Take notes. Challenge decisions if something doesn't seem right. And most importantly—pray. Never stop praying."

Tears filled their eyes as they listened. One woman hugged me tightly. "Thank you," she whispered, "I needed to hear that."

As night fell, I checked on Robert one last time. His eyes were clearer now, the redness fading. Another sign of God's power at work.

While he rested, I pulled out my laptop and started researching the therapy programs he would soon begin. Physical, occupational, and speech therapy would all play a role in his recovery. I wanted to be prepared, to understand what lay ahead so I could continue advocating for him every step of the way.

The Monnity Miracle

After my research, I closed my laptop and whispered a prayer over Robert.

God, thank You for bringing us this far. I trust You to guide us through the next steps. You have shown Your power, and I believe greater things are still to come.

As I settled into the chair for the night, a deep peace washed over me.

Robert's journey wasn't over. But neither was God's plan.

And I knew—with absolute certainty—that the best was yet to come.

God's Promise

I can do all this through him who gives me strength.
Philippians 4:13

There is no scenario or condition that you cannot conquer. If you have faith in God, He will provide you with the strength to accomplish whatever you need to achieve. I understand that, at times, the task appears unachievable, but it isn't if you turn to God and seek His help.

A New Plan for Recovery

At 6:00 a.m., my phone alarm rang, but I was already awake. My heart raced with excitement—Robert was awake. After days of praying, believing, and refusing to give up, today felt like the first step toward his full recovery. I couldn't wait to hear what the doctors would say, to see what progress he would make. I jumped up, hurried through my morning routine, and rushed back to his bedside, eager to embrace whatever miracles the day would bring.

I gently touched his forehead, and he slowly opened his eyes. "I'm trusting God to do something amazing for us today," I whispered, holding his hand. He stared at me, his eyes filled with awareness, as I prayed over him and the day ahead.

Shortly after, the doctor arrived with the therapy team. Today was a big day. The doctor would be reviewing Robert's medication list, and the therapy team would present their plan for his recovery.

"Good morning, Mrs. Monnity," he greeted warmly.

"Good morning to you," I responded.

He turned his attention to Robert, "Mr. Monnity, how are you today? Blink once for bad, twice for good."

Robert blinked twice.

"Your vitals look stable, but your blood pressure is a little high. I'm going to prescribe Lisinopril to help regulate it. This will aid in reducing your blood pressure since we aim to encourage you to start moving as quickly as we can."

65

The Monnity Miracle

As he reviewed Robert's medications, I made a mental note to research Lisinopril. I had never heard of it before and wanted to ensure it was the best choice for Robert.

The doctor then introduced the therapy team, each specialist stepping forward to explain their role.

The physical therapist stepped up to Robert's bedside, her demeanor warm yet professional. Gently, she helped him sit up, carefully supporting his movements. His eyes locked onto her, attentive despite the strain of the effort.

"How are you today?" she asked, her voice clear and encouraging, "Blink once for bad and twice for good."

Robert blinked twice.

A smile spread across her face, "That's great! I'm your physical therapist, and I'm here to help you regain your mobility and get back on your feet. How does that sound?"

Again, Robert blinked twice.

"Excellent!" she said, "Let's start with a strength test." She extended her hand, "Squeeze my finger as hard as you can."

Robert gripped her finger, his hold surprisingly firm.

"Well done," she praised, "You're showing resilience, and that's a good sign."

Next, she instructed him to move each of his legs individually. He managed slight movements, though they were weak and unsteady.

The Monnity Miracle

"That's okay," she reassured him, "This is exactly why I'm here—to assess where you are so we can build from here."

Finally, she raised her hand a few inches above his leg. "Try lifting your leg to touch my hand," she encouraged.

Robert attempted the movement, struggling but determined.

She nodded, "That's a great start. Don't worry; we'll work on building your strength little by little."

Stepping back, she met his gaze, "You did really well today. I'll see you tomorrow, and we'll take the next step together."

Next, the occupational therapist explained how she would help him relearn essential daily tasks like dressing, eating, and maintaining balance.

"We'll get started once your intubation tube is removed."

Finally, the speech therapist stepped forward.

"I'm here to help you regain communication. I look forward to working with you soon."

I thanked them all as they left, reassured that we had a strong team guiding Robert's recovery.

The Power of Advocacy and Prayer

About an hour later, the nurse entered to administer Robert's medication.

The Monnity Miracle

"Mrs. Monnity, I just wanted to mention—Lisinopril can have some serious side effects, especially for African Americans," he said hesitantly.

My heart sank, "What kind of side effects?"

I quickly pulled out my laptop and typed "Lisinopril side effects" into Google. As I scanned the list, my stomach tightened.

- Muscle cramps
- Tiredness
- Vomiting
- Problems with urination
- Abdominal pain
- Blurry vision
- Sweating
- Skin rash
- Swollen lips (particularly in African Americans)

My heart sank. Robert had already endured so much—how could I risk adding these potential complications? The uncertainty gnawed at me. Would this medication truly help him, or would it introduce a new set of challenges?

I thanked the nurse for alerting me and made a note to watch Robert closely for any reactions.

Stepping to Robert's bedside, I whispered a prayer:

"Lord, I trust You. If this medication isn't right, please reveal it to us. Let it do no harm. Cover Robert in Your healing power. In Jesus' name, Amen."

The Monnity Miracle

Just as I finished, a knock came at the door. It was the respiratory specialist.

"Mrs. Monnity, you're still here," he noted with a smile.

"I'm not going anywhere," I replied, "I'll leave when my husband walks out of here with me."

He nodded, checking the machines. Moments later, he looked up at me with a grin.

"Well, your prayers have been answered. Based on these numbers, we can begin testing to take him off the ventilator."

I shot up from my chair, "Thank You, Jesus!"

I leaned over Robert. "Sweet P, I believe tomorrow you'll be breathing on your own," I told him. His eyes were glossy but clear, locked onto mine. Hope filled the room.

I sent out a praise report to our family and friends: *God is moving! Keep praying—Robert's ventilator may come out tomorrow!*

Standing in Faith for Tomorrow

Throughout the day, visitors streamed in, offering encouragement. Some were amazed by Robert's progress; others simply expressed admiration for my unwavering faith.

"Tyra, we know this hasn't been easy for you," one relative said, "But your faithfulness to Robert is inspiring."

69

The Monnity Miracle

"I appreciate that, but all the glory belongs to God. He's given me the strength to stand."

As the evening set in, visiting hours ended, and the room grew quiet. I sat in my chair, reflecting on the day. Everything was aligning—God was orchestrating Robert's healing step by step.

Tomorrow was a big day. I prayed that the Lisinopril would work without complications, that the respiratory specialist would move forward with removing the ventilator, and that the therapy team would finalize a plan to help Robert regain his strength.

Checking on Robert one last time, I whispered, "No matter what, we're going to get through this. I'm fighting for you on this side, and I need you to keep fighting on yours."

With that, I finally drifted off to sleep, resting in the certainty that God was not finished yet.

God's Promise

The Lord sustains him on his sickbed;
in his illness you restore him to full health.

Psalm 41:3

Regardless of the illness or condition you are enduring, God can entirely and wholly return you to perfect health. This indicates that even if you are confined to a sickbed. God continues to perform miracles. Nothing is too hard for God when you have faith.

Rehabilitation

I woke up before my alarm, the weight of anticipation pressing on my mind. Today was a critical day—Robert might be taken off the ventilator, we would find out if the Lisinopril was effective, and we would learn the extent of his therapy.

I stood up from my chair and walked over to check on Robert. To my shock, his lips were swollen—just like the images I had seen online. They looked like two hot air balloons. My heart pounded as I immediately called the nurse. When he arrived, he examined Robert and said, "This is the side effect of the Lisinopril I mentioned yesterday."

I didn't hesitate. "Please call the doctor," I said firmly, "And do not give him that medication this morning until I speak with him." I turned back to Robert and softly asked, "Are you in any pain?" He blinked once—no.

"At least you're not in pain," I reassured him. But my mind was racing.

A few moments later, Robert started coughing. Alarmed, I called the nurse again and asked him to contact respiratory therapy. I knew vomiting was another side effect of Lisinopril, and I didn't want Robert to aspirate. Within minutes, my fears became reality—he began to vomit.

The nurse rushed back in, quickly elevating Robert's bed to prevent choking. "Hold on, we're going to help you," I told Robert, my heart pounding. The nurse slipped on gloves and gently cleaned his mouth.

The Monnity Miracle

Shortly after, the doctor arrived. I pointed at Robert's lips. "We need to stop giving him Lisinopril immediately," I insisted, "This is not working for him."

The doctor examined Robert carefully. "I completely agree, Mrs. Monnity," he said, "We'll switch him to Hydralazine instead and monitor his response."

For now, Robert seemed stable. The doctor assured me he would check back later. As the nurse stepped in to clean up and change Robert's gown, he informed me that the therapy team and respiratory therapy would be arriving soon.

A Breakthrough Moment

The respiratory therapist arrived first. "Good morning, Mrs. Monnity," he greeted me warmly, "How are you today?"

I nodded, distracted as I typed *Hydralazine* into my laptop, researching its potential side effects.

He ran his tests, then looked up with a smile, "I have great news— his numbers are strong enough to remove the ventilator today."

I froze, "Wait, can you repeat that?"

He chuckled, "Robert is ready to be taken off the ventilator. His oxygen levels look great."

My heart leaped. "Thank You, Jesus!" I whispered.

"You've been praying for this, haven't you?" he asked, smiling.

The Monnity Miracle

"Yes," I said, tears welling in my eyes, "My God is so good."

He stepped out to call the doctor. I bent down to Robert's ear. "You're going to be able to talk again soon," I whispered. He stared at me, then, for the first time, nodded instead of blinking.

Moments later, the therapy team arrived, their energy high. "Good morning!" one of them said cheerfully, "We hear Robert is coming off the ventilator today!"

"That's right," I said, smiling.

"That's excellent," the physical therapist responded, "That means we can get him sitting up in a chair for a couple of hours today."

"Do you always move patients so fast?" I asked, surprised.

"Not always," she explained, "Each case is different, but in Robert's case, he's alert and strong enough for us to start helping him regain mobility."

The respiratory therapist returned, "The doctor is on the way to remove his ventilator."

The therapy team stepped back, and I took Robert's hand as the doctor arrived and explained the process. A nurse assisted as they wheeled Robert out of the room.

Thirty minutes later, Robert was back. The tube was out.

"There were no complications," the doctor assured me, "His throat may be sore for a few days, and his voice might sound hoarse, but that's temporary."

Robert now wore an oxygen mask but looked comfortable. I leaned in. "How do you feel?" I asked.

Robert gave me a thumbs-up.

Defying Expectations

As Robert rested, the therapy team returned. Seeing him sitting up, they beamed. "Robert, are you ready to start?" the physical therapist asked.

With a voice barely above a whisper, he said, "Yes."

It was raspy, almost like Scooby-Doo, but it was his voice.

The nurse brought in a lift to help move him to the chair. The physical therapist smiled. "You're going to spend some time here today," she told him, "Tomorrow, we'll work on standing and walking."

The speech therapist joined in, "I know you just had your tube out, so I won't ask too much of you today. But can you do me a favor and tell me your name?"

Slowly, Robert whispered, "Robert."

She grinned, "That's all I needed to hear."

As this was happening, I caught movement in the hallway. A familiar figure passed by the open door, hesitated and stepped back.

The Monnity Miracle

I turned. It was the ER doctor—the one who had told me nine days ago that my husband was brain-dead.

She stared, eyes wide, mouth slightly open. Then she stammered, "Is that… the same man from the ER?"

I smiled, tears threatening to spill over. "Yes," I said proudly, "And he is alive and well. Thank You, Jesus."

She was speechless. For nearly a minute, she just stood there, staring. Then, without another word, she turned and walked away, shaking her head.

I turned back to Robert, beaming with pride.

The occupational therapist pulled out a small bag filled with colorful cups. "Robert," she said, placing them on the table, "I want you to restack these cups from one side to the other."

Slowly, deliberately, Robert reached for the first cup.

One by one, he moved them, each motion a victory.

"Great job, Robert!" the therapist encouraged, "I can tell you're up for a challenge tomorrow."

Robert tilted his head slightly in agreement.

The therapy team huddled for a few minutes before returning to me. "We're really pleased with his progress today," one said, "Here's our plan for tomorrow: we'll work on his balance and start walking with a gait belt and walker."

The Monnity Miracle

"Will I be able to attend his sessions?" I asked.

"Of course," they assured me.

"Good," I said, "He needs to know I'm right here every step of the way."

Gratitude and Praise

After they left, the nurse returned to check Robert's vitals.

"His lips are already going down," I observed.

"Yes," the nurse agreed, "And his blood pressure is excellent—128/62. Looks like the Hydralazine is working."

Tears filled my eyes. "Thank You, Jesus!" I whispered.

After updating Robert's medication chart, I picked up my phone and sent out a *Praise Report* to family and friends. Within minutes, my phone buzzed with replies:

"Won't He do it!"
"Praise God!"
"We serve a miracle-working God!"

I later learned that entire churches had been praying for us, with intercessors keeping a 24-hour prayer watch for Robert's recovery.

That night, as visiting hours ended and the hospital quieted, I sat beside Robert, watching him rest peacefully.

The Monnity Miracle

I leaned in and whispered, "You did so well today. I am so proud of you."

As I sat back in my chair and closed my eyes, I knew—tomorrow would be another step toward the miracle God was unfolding before us.

God's Promise

"When the time is right, I, the Lord, will make it happen"
Isaiah 60:22

God has a set time for everything. He is never too early, nor is he too late. At the appointed time, He will make things happen.

Second Chance at Life & Recovery

This morning, I awoke to sunlight streaming through the window in Robert's room. The sun was shining exceptionally bright. I got up and headed straight to the restroom, trying not to disturb Robert, who was sleeping soundly. As I walked down the hallway, I noticed that the patient in the room next to Robert had passed away. The housekeeping staff was in the room, mopping the floor, sanitizing the surfaces with disinfectant wipes, and collecting the trash.

With concern in my voice, I asked, "What happened to him?" The housekeeper, speaking softly, replied, "He has died, and that's why I'm here preparing the room for the next patient."

I mentioned that I had never seen anyone visit him. The housekeeper responded, "I noticed the same thing, but I can't say anything to anyone because it's not my business." I expressed my frustration, "It's unfortunate that nobody came to see him. Perhaps if someone had been there, it could have made a difference in his survival." She agreed with me, and I apologized for interrupting her work. I was just concerned because when I looked through the window, I no longer saw him in the bed.

"No problem," she said, "I understand."

After freshening up in the restroom, I returned to Robert's room, feeling a bit disheartened. I tried to hide my emotions as I walked in. I quickly took out my notepad, made a note about the patient's passing, and said a prayer for him and his family.

The Monnity Miracle

While I waited for Robert to wake up, I reflected on the situation and wondered what would have happened if I hadn't been there for Robert. He could have found himself in the same lonely situation, but thankfully, that wasn't the case. I thanked God for blessing me with a fighting spirit and for strengthening me during these difficult moments.

I realized that not everyone is a warrior, and I was deeply grateful to God for giving me the courage to face challenges with bravery. As the Bible says in 2 Timothy 1:7, "For God has not given us a spirit of fear, but of power, love, and a sound mind." I know that when you or your loved ones face traumatic situations, it can feel overwhelming and intimidating. But this is where your connection with God becomes crucial. He is your rock and foundation, and no one is greater than Him. God means the world to me.

I poured out my gratitude to God, not only for everything He has done but also for what He will continue to do for Robert. I closed my notepad and said, "Amen."

Before long, I heard Robert stirring in the bed and greeted him, "Good morning!" This time, instead of giving me a thumbs-up, he tried to speak and said, "Good morning, Chica!" I smiled and responded, "Oh yes, you are returning to your old self." "Chica" was a nickname he used to call me before his stroke.

I told him the doctor and nurse would be arriving soon to evaluate his condition and provide his medication. I mentioned that the swelling in his lips had decreased a bit more. I asked if he was feeling any discomfort. In his best Scooby-Doo voice, he replied, "No!" I smiled, as I'm a big fan of Scooby-Doo.

The Monnity Miracle

At that moment, the doctor entered and started reviewing the notes from the previous day before discussing the plans for the day. He noticed that Robert's vital signs were stable, and the Hydralazine medication appeared to be working well, with no side effects at the moment. "So, we'll keep him on this," the doctor said.

Turning to Robert, he asked, "How are you doing?"

Robert replied, "Alright!"

The doctor also noticed that Robert's voice sounded a little off, but this was expected after the removal of the breathing tube. At that point, the nurse interjected, saying, "Respiratory will be in shortly."

"Alright," the doctor responded.

The doctor then examined Robert's eyes, noting that they had improved significantly since a few days ago. Everything seemed fine. Robert was breathing on his own; he could sit up in bed by himself, and his vital signs looked excellent. The doctor, seeing Robert's significant progress, said, "I'm going to place an order this morning to transfer him from the ICU to a standard room."

I sat up straight in my chair. "What did you say?" I asked.

The doctor repeated, "I recommend transferring Robert from the ICU to a standard room because of his considerable improvement."

I couldn't contain my excitement, "Thank You, Lord! Thank You, Lord! Now You are really showing off, God!"

The Monnity Miracle

The doctor looked at me and said, "This case has really defined my career. I've never seen anything like it."

I thanked the doctor for all his help, and he responded, "You and Mr. Monnity are very welcome." He asked if I had any questions.

"Yes!" I said, "When can we take off the oxygen mask?"

The doctor explained that the respiratory team would be able to answer that question better than he could and would let me know soon whether Robert could have the mask removed that day.

As I sat in the chair and waited for the news about Robert's room transfer, my mind turned to the goodness of God. I couldn't help but marvel at all that God was accomplishing and the speed with which He was doing it. I felt a deep sense of admiration for His work. I began to pray for the new room we were about to move into, asking God to keep blessing the medication Robert was on, to heal his body with divine intervention, and to send us the right staff with the right attitude and mindset. It was so important to have patience when learning to "relearn" anything. I also prayed for the success of Robert's therapy sessions that day. As I prayed, the verse from Philippians 4:6 came to mind: "Do not be anxious about anything, but in every situation, by prayer and petition, with thanksgiving, present your requests to God." I expressed my gratitude, trusting that God was already working in Robert's life. In faith, I prayed in the name of Jesus, amen.

When I approached Robert's bed, I asked, "How are you feeling?" He replied, "Alright!" I smiled and asked, "Are you excited about your therapy sessions today?" He answered, "Yes, for the most part." I mentioned that the therapy team would be arriving soon.

The Monnity Miracle

Just then, the nurse came in with great news. "Mr. and Mrs. Monnity, we have a room ready for you. The transport will arrive in 15 minutes." I said, "That was quick!" The nurse explained that the doctor had submitted the request this morning, and a room was already available. "Thank You, God!" I asked, "What about his therapy sessions?" The nurse reassured me, "The therapy team has been notified of your room change and will see you there." I replied, "I really appreciate it." Turning to Robert, I said, "God is great!" He agreed, "Yes, He is."

A Day of Progress

As I began to gather my belongings, there was a knock at the door. Several doctors and nurses were standing there, ready to wish Robert well. They shared how amazed they were by his recovery and mentioned that they had been inspired by his situation. One nurse remarked, "We've been talking about you both since your arrival. We've seen God do incredible things in this room. We just wanted to wish Mr. Monnity a speedy recovery." Another nurse added, "Mrs. Monnity, you've been here day and night by Robert's side. We admire your strength. You've supported us through some challenges in your own life, and we are truly grateful." I replied, "Thank you for everything you've done for us. We couldn't have done it without your help." I hugged each of them as they left the room.

Moments later, the transporter, Michael, arrived. "Hi, I'm Michael. I'll be taking Mr. Monnity to his new room. Are you ready to go?" We replied, "Yes!" Michael checked that everything was in order before confirming, "All set! Let's go!" As we walked down the corridor, we passed other families in the ICU who wished us well. "May God bless you and your husband," one person said. I responded, "Thank you! I wish everything goes well for your loved ones, too."

We made our way to the elevator, and just a few minutes later, we arrived at Robert's new room. The therapy team and nursing staff were already there, waiting for us. They gave us about 20 minutes to settle in. The nurse introduced herself and wrote her name on the whiteboard. Then, the therapy team greeted us warmly. There was a new member, Tony, who was a physical therapist. He introduced himself and began by getting Robert ready for a standing exercise. He put a gait belt around Robert's waist to help him stand. Slowly, with Tony's help, Robert got to his feet, though a little unsteady. Tony encouraged him, "You're doing great, Robert!" After walking a few steps forward, Tony noticed that Robert's legs were scissoring and explained that this would improve with time and therapy.

They continued walking down the hall and then turned back toward the room. I cheered Robert on, "You've got this, honey!" Back in the room, Tony helped Robert sit on the chair, checking his upper body strength. He asked, "How are you feeling?" Robert answered, "I'm fine." After about 10 minutes of standing and sitting exercises, Tony concluded, "You did great today, Robert. Keep up the good work. It'll take time, but we'll get there."

Next, the speech therapist arrived. She smiled at Robert and said, "I know we didn't talk much last time, but today we'll do some exercises together." They began with breathing exercises to improve Robert's breath support and control. After a few minutes, the therapist asked, "Can I ask you a few questions?" Robert agreed. She asked for his name, the year, his location, and even his birthday to assess his cognitive abilities. When she asked about his wife, Robert proudly said, "Tyra." She smiled and said, "You're doing great, Robert. Let's keep going." Though Robert's voice was still a bit hoarse, he was making progress.

After speech therapy, the occupational therapist came in. She set up a cup stacking exercise to improve Robert's hand-eye coordination. "Let's see how well you can do this," she encouraged. Robert carefully stacked the cups, and after several repetitions, she praised him, "Great job, Robert! Keep practicing, and your coordination will improve." He smiled at me, and I gave him a thumbs up.

As the therapist stood up to join the others on the opposite side of the room, they gathered for about 10 minutes. While we chatted, I turned to Robert and told him how proud I was of him. He smiled and said, "Thank you very much, Chica." Soon, the team approached Robert's bed and shared their observations from the past two days. Based on their assessment, they recommended that Robert be sent to a rehabilitation center to continue his physical, speech, and occupational therapy. They were impressed by his progress and hoped to see him advance even further. They assured us they would inform the doctor of their recommendation and work with the nurse to find a nearby rehabilitation center so we wouldn't have to travel too far. This news felt like a weight had been lifted off our shoulders. I looked at Robert and said, "We'll be leaving shortly for rehab." He nodded, "Alright!" I then asked the therapy team, "When can we depart?" They replied, "Once we secure a bed at the facility." They asked if I had any further questions, and I responded, "No, but I appreciate your help." They smiled and said, "It's been a pleasure to work with you both. Mr. Monnity, we wish you the best of success." Robert simply said, "Thank you."

The Monnity Miracle

A few moments later, the nurse entered with Robert's medication. The therapy team informed her of their suggestion for Robert to transfer to a rehabilitation center. The nurse asked me, "Is there a particular area you're familiar with?" I replied, "What about Laurel?" She responded, "I'll check into that for you." She then approached Robert and said, "Mr. Monnity, I need to check your vitals and administer your medication." He responded, "Alright." As the blood pressure monitor beeped, I asked, "What's his blood pressure?" The nurse replied, "It's 134/70." I quietly said, "Thank You, Lord." I turned to Robert and asked, "Isn't that good, honey?" He answered, "Yes, it is." I then asked, "How are you feeling after all the therapy today?" He replied, "Great!" Robert has never been one to say much, but when he speaks, you know exactly what he means.

The nurse took a while to return with information about the Laurel Rehabilitation Center, so I began to pray for guidance. It was crucial to find a nearby center, especially since I would be driving there daily until Robert returned home. I sat quietly in my chair, closed my eyes, and prayed: "Lord, in Jesus' name, I ask that You guide us to the Laurel Rehabilitation Center if it aligns with Your will. If there's a better place, please show it to me, and we will go there. I ask for kindness, grace, and compassion, knowing that nothing is too difficult for You, Lord. Please provide us with the right location, the right therapists, and the right mindset for Robert's recovery. I surrender all the plans for his rehabilitation into Your hands. In Jesus' name, amen."

Not long after, the nurse returned with good news: they had a bed available at the Laurel Rehabilitation Center, and Robert would be transported there in a butler instead of an ambulance. I was overjoyed! "This is perfect!" I stood and leaned over Robert's bed, saying, "We got you a bed, and we'll be leaving soon." He smiled and replied, "That sounds good to me." While we waited for the butler to arrive, I gathered my bags and sat down to send out a "Praise Report" to our family and friends, letting them know Robert was being transferred to the rehabilitation center to continue his recovery. My phone was instantly filled with excited responses. I promised to send another update once we were settled in. Their support meant the world to us.

Soon, the nurse returned with Michael, the transport driver, who was ready to take us downstairs to the butler. We thanked the nursing staff as we left. We rode the elevator one last time, and as they rolled Robert outside and loaded him into the butler, I asked the driver if I could follow behind. He agreed, and we set off. The drive took about 45 minutes, though the rush-hour traffic on Baltimore Ave made it feel longer.

When we arrived, we were greeted by the nursing staff. I was told that all of Robert's medical documentation had already been sent over from the hospital. Unfortunately, there wasn't a private room available, but we made the best of it. Robert's room was clean and had a beautiful bay window. I asked the nurse if I could stay the night, but she informed me there was no space for visitors. I asked, "What's the earliest I can come back tomorrow?" She replied, "8:00 AM." I said, "Okay, I'll be back then." I leaned over to Robert and said, "Sorry, honey, I can't stay with you tonight. I'll be back in the morning." Robert jokingly patted the bed and said, "You can stay right here." I laughed and told him, "You're sweet, but that twin bed isn't big enough for both of us."

Just then, the doctor entered. "Hello, I'm Dr. Bruce Neckritz. It's a pleasure to meet you both." I replied, "Pleasure to meet you too,

Dr. Neckritz." Robert greeted him, "Hi, Doc!" Dr. Neckritz explained that he had reviewed Robert's medical information and suggested that Robert receive one hour of physical, occupational, and speech therapy each day for five days a week. I asked if I could be present during all of Robert's therapy sessions, and he assured me, "Certainly, you can." He then led us to the activity room, where Robert would receive his physical and occupational therapy. The nurse brought a wheelchair, as Robert was still too unstable to walk on his own. Dr. Neckritz showed us the room where Robert would have speech therapy and mentioned, "You can meet with all the therapists in the morning. Many of them have already left for the day." We returned to Robert's room, settled in, and the doctor left. The nurse came back to inform us that Robert would receive his final medication at 9:00 PM. I said, "Alright, thanks for letting us know." We sat together for a while, watching TV. I told Robert I would bring him some clothes tomorrow, and he responded, "Alright!" Shortly after, the nurse returned with his medication, signaling that it was time for me to go. I kissed Robert goodnight and told him, "I'll see you in the morning."

A Revelation and a Praise

It has been a very long day but one full of progress and promise. On my way home, I reflected on all the blessings God had given us that day, feeling so grateful for everything that had come together. Robert was doing so well, and it was truly amazing. My heart was full of thankfulness, knowing that soon, he'd be back home with me.

I started to pray: "God, please cover Robert with Your blood, send Your angels to watch over him tonight, and thank You for everything You've done for us today. Thank You for all the therapists, for Robert's room, for the butler who made sure Robert was safely transported to the rehab center, and for the medication that's finally working for him. We pray that he rests peacefully tonight. All the glory and praise go to You. I pray this in the name of Jesus, Amen."

God's Promise

Be still, and know that I am God.

Psalm 46:10

We must understand that God is in control of every situation in our life.

The Home Stretch

The next morning, waking up at home in my own bed felt unusual after spending the last 14 days sleeping in a chair. It was around 6:30 AM when I glanced at the clock, and immediately, I remembered the nurse's words, "The soonest I can get there is 8:00 AM." I quickly jumped out of bed, knelt down, and began my prayer.

"Lord, we welcome You into this day. We offer You praise and honor, expressing, 'Thank You, Lord, for another new day.' We entrust this day to You, asking that You guide our path. I pray that Robert had a restful night and wakes up feeling strong and prepared for his therapy session today. Empower Robert, Comfort Robert, Support Robert, and shield him. Please assist the therapists in being patient with him, and may he have a wonderful day. In the name of Jesus, I pray. Amen."

I then grabbed my phone. In the excitement of helping Robert settle into the rehab center, I had forgotten to send the text with his details. I quickly shared the Praise Report along with the visiting hours. My phone buzzed with messages of gratitude. I got up, washed up, and got dressed. Soon, I was on my way to the rehab center. It was early, so there was little traffic, and I arrived quickly.

As I exited the elevator and walked by the front desk, I greeted, "Good morning to all!" They responded, "Hello," and asked me to stop at the desk. I told them I was there to visit my husband, Mr. Monnity. The nurse looked up his details, gave me a visitor pass, and instructed me to wear it on my shirt. I responded, "Alright, enjoy your day!" and made my way to Robert's room.

The Monnity Miracle

I arrived at his room at 7:30 AM, gave him his clothes, and greeted him with, "Good morning, sweetheart." He responded, "Good morning, Chica." I helped him into his wheelchair and wheeled him into the bathroom. He managed to brush his teeth and wash his face on his own, but getting dressed was a bit challenging. So, I helped him get dressed. Shortly after, he was back in his wheelchair, ready to go.

As we left the bathroom, the nurse entered with his medication but needed to check his vital signs first. He extended his arm, and she placed the blood pressure cuff on his arm. After pressing a button on the blood pressure monitor, we heard the beep sound. His blood pressure was stable at 135/72.

She asked, "Is he ready for therapy today?" He responded, "Yes!" She gave him his medication, and breakfast was brought in. While he ate, Dr. Neckritz entered, accompanied by the therapists. "Good morning, Mr. Monnity," the doctor said. "How's your morning going?" Robert replied, "Great!" Dr. Neckritz continued, "I've organized for your therapy team to meet with you. This is Terry, the physical therapist, Ellen, the occupational therapist, and Jenn, the speech therapist." Everyone greeted Robert, and Dr. Neckritz said, "The lovely lady beside him is his wife. She'll accompany him to all his therapy sessions." They all responded, "The more, the better!" I smiled and said, "It's great to meet you all."

Ellen led the way, saying, "Now that we've made introductions, let's start with occupational therapy." She pushed Robert into the activity room and handed him two ten-pound weights to enhance his upper body strength. She gave him five different weight exercises, which he did for about fifteen minutes. Afterward, Ellen showed him how to take his socks on and off. This continued for another fifteen minutes. She then said, "Robert, you did great today."

Next, Terry approached for physical therapy. He put a gait belt on Robert and instructed him to stand up and walk around the edge of the activity room. Robert felt a bit unsteady, but Terry reassured me that he was fine. He walked for ten minutes before taking a five-minute break. Then, he walked and bounced a large yellow ball with Terry supporting him. This went on for another ten minutes before he was placed on the resistance machine. After ten minutes, Terry told Robert he could sit down and rest. He reassured him that he was doing well and would continue to grow stronger.

I wheeled Robert back to his room, and he lay down on the bed, mentioning that his arms and legs hurt a little. I explained that it was normal, but the pain should go away in a few days.

A few hours later, Jenn, the speech therapist, arrived for his 1:00 PM session. She had Robert practice articulation exercises for clearer sounds, tongue movements for coordination, and breathing exercises for better voice control. She explained that in future sessions, he'd work on voice quality exercises like humming, word games to improve vocabulary, and conversation practice to enhance communication skills in everyday life.

Jenn finished the session by saying, "Robert, keep up the great effort, and I'll see you tomorrow." Robert replied, "Alright, I'll see you tomorrow." I wheeled him back to his room, and lunch was served. He ate and reclined, clearly tired. I kept quiet to let him rest. As the day wound down, I sat quietly in a chair and whispered a small prayer, "Thank You, Lord. It's great to see Robert standing and growing stronger each day. Thank You, God. We are incredibly grateful. I pray in Jesus' name. Amen."

Suddenly, my phone buzzed. Some of our family and friends wanted to visit Robert. I provided them with the rehab center's address, and a few hours later, they arrived. We met in the family room and chatted for a bit, but Robert was still recovering his energy from the earlier physical therapy session. He was happy to see his family and friends, and after about 20 minutes, they said their goodbyes and wished him well.

I wheeled Robert back to his room and then sat down to watch TV for a while. It was time for the evening meal. After dinner, Robert relaxed and soon fell asleep. At 9:30 PM, I woke him up to take his medication, and I didn't want to leave without saying goodbye.

The following three days followed the same routine. Then, on July 4th, Dr. Neckritz visited Robert. He shared that the therapy team believed Robert was doing excellently and that his strong support system (me) had played a big part in his progress. The doctor added, "I believe you're ready to go home." Robert smiled widely and said, "Thanks, Doc." I said, "Dr. Neckritz, I appreciate you and your team for everything." He replied, "You're welcome, Mrs. Monnity. But before I can discharge him, I have to explain a few things."

I said, "What do we need to do?"

The Monnity Miracle

Dr. Neckritz explained:

1. Avoid unnecessary stress and stressful conversations. Robert needs to stay calm.
2. Get plenty of rest. Don't try to do too much too soon—his body needs to heal.
3. Exercise every day for 15 minutes, such as walking outside or on a treadmill, to strengthen the heart.
4. Take medication on time and consistently, with no excuses.
5. Keep regular doctor's appointments. Don't skip them.
6. Eat a balanced diet—no processed foods, foods high in salt, canned soups, cookies, candy, or alcohol.
7. Listen to his body. If he's tired or fatigued, rest.
8. Drink plenty of water.
9. Continue therapy with an outpatient rehab center near home for 6 weeks.
10. Keep a daily log of medication, noting the date and time it's taken.

The doctor asked, "Do you have any questions?" We both replied, "No!" He then said, "Excuse me, I need to place the discharge order."

The Final Sessions

The nurse entered to administer Robert's medication and check his vitals. Even though we were being discharged, we still needed to finish his final three therapy sessions. After Robert took his medication, Jonas arrived to take him to physical therapy.

The Monnity Miracle

When they entered the activity room, Robert saw Troy, a man who had also experienced a stroke and was unable to move his left side. We had seen him in physical therapy several times. Troy turned to Robert and said, "I see you working so hard every day. You've motivated me to give it my best effort, too. When I first came here, I was feeling sorry for myself, but seeing you work so hard changed my mindset. Now I'm putting in the effort to reunite with my family." He then told his therapist that he wanted to try walking without the walker. Not only did he walk unaided, but he also made two laps around the activity room without getting winded.

Robert encouraged him, "Keep pushing forward and trust in God. You'll get out of here and return to your family." Troy turned to me and asked, "Are you his wife?" I replied, "Yes." He said, "I admire you for standing by him. I see you here every day with him. You're a wonderful wife." I thanked him for his kind words.

Jonas returned, and Robert began his session. He did three sets of leg lifts and walked around the room confidently, no longer swaying. Jonas cheered him on, saying, "You've got this, Robert." After his final lap, he sat back down in his wheelchair. Jonas praised him, "Well done, Robert! You're doing great!"

Next, Jenn arrived for speech therapy. Robert's progress in speech was impressive. He was doing so much better compared to just five days ago. She concluded the session by having Robert read aloud. "Great work, Robert; you've done exceptionally well." Just as she finished, lunch was being served. I rolled Robert back to his room, knowing we had four hours until his occupational therapy session.

The Monnity Miracle

Curious if we could step outside, I asked the nurse, and she enthusiastically replied, "Yes!" Taking advantage of the beautiful weather, we wheeled Robert out to soak in the sunlight and fresh air. It was a perfect day.

For nearly two hours, we enjoyed the outdoors, but the warmth of the sun eventually wore Robert out. We returned to his room, where he lay down for a much-needed nap. Before long, it was time for his final therapy session. Ellen encouraged Robert to get up, and together, they worked on puzzles, strength exercises, and balance training. You should have seen him—I was so proud of his progress. He stood on his own two feet, a testament to how far he had come.

As the session ended, Ellen praised Robert's determination. "Keep up the great work," she encouraged. "You'll be back to your old self soon." She wished him well, and I led him outside once more. This time, we found ourselves in a gazebo.

And then, in that sacred space, Robert stood independently for the first time in twenty-one days. It was a breathtaking moment—watching him rise, reclaiming his strength, and embracing the miracles God had worked in his life. Tears of joy streamed down my face as I witnessed his unwavering fight for recovery. We leaned on God completely, every single day, because we knew—without a doubt—He is still in the healing business.

My phone rang—it was Robert's friend, Pastor DeeKee. I answered and shared the good news: "Robert will be released tomorrow." Excited, Pastor DeeKee said he wanted to visit. "Of course!" I told him, "You can come by tomorrow."

The Monnity Miracle

He asked to speak with Robert, so I passed him the phone. Their conversation lasted about ten minutes before they exchanged goodbyes. "I'll see you tomorrow," Pastor DeeKee assured him.

Shortly after, the nurse entered the room with an update. "Robert, your discharge paperwork has been processed for tomorrow," she announced with a warm smile. We both thanked her sincerely. "We truly appreciate all of your help."

To pass the time, we played a few rounds of *Uno*. Laughter filled the room as we enjoyed the game, but before long, Robert began to feel sleepy. He laid down to rest while I watched TV for a couple of hours.

Eventually, it was time for me to head home. Leaving Robert there for one last night was tough, but knowing he'd be coming home tomorrow filled me with relief. As I gathered my things, the nurse came in with his medication.

"Good night, honey," I said kindly, "I'll see you tomorrow."

Going Home

The morning light streamed through the window as I opened my eyes, my heart already overflowing with praise. Before my feet touched the floor, I lifted my hands and began worshiping God, thanking Him for all He had done for Robert. Tears welled in my eyes as I reflected on the magnitude of this moment.

"Lord, You are the greatest," I whispered through my tears.

I knew not every family had been as fortunate as we were. Over the past few weeks, I had witnessed families leaving the hospital with broken hearts for their loved ones not surviving. Yet here we were—Robert was going home.

"Thank You, Lord, for Your kindness, grace, and compassion," I prayed, "You orchestrated this entire process. Thank You for the medical insurance that allowed Robert to receive the best possible care. Thank You for every doctor, nurse, and specialist who played a role in his healing. And thank You, Lord, for our family and friends who stood by us through this trial. This journey revealed who our true supporters were, and for that, I am grateful."

This was bigger than us. The Monnity Miracle had impacted countless lives—some we knew about and others we would never meet. But today, I stood in awe of God's faithfulness.

"You promised he would live and not die, and today, You are bringing him home," I declared, "Thank You for keeping Your word, Lord. Now, as we take this step forward, please guide us. We give everything to You, Lord, because I know I cannot do this without You."

With that, I ended my prayer, whispering, "In Jesus' name, Amen."

Preparing for the Homecoming

I stepped into the shower, allowing the warm water to soothe the emotions surging through me. After getting dressed, I grabbed my handbag and keys, eager to get to the rehabilitation center early in case any final paperwork needed to be completed.

The drive was smooth, and I arrived quicker than expected. I even found a parking spot right in front of the building—perfect for ensuring Robert wouldn't have to walk far on his first day out of rehab.

As I walked through the main entrance, several nurses greeted me with bright smiles.

"Good morning, Mrs. Monnity!" one of them called out.

"Good morning, ladies," I replied warmly.

When I reached Robert's room, I could hear the nurse speaking with him. As I stepped inside, she was checking his vitals and preparing his morning medication.

"Good morning!" I greeted cheerfully.

"Good morning, dear!" she responded.

Robert turned his head toward me and grinned. "Hey, Chica! Good morning!"

I laughed, "Are you ready to get out of here?"

"Yes! I've been ready!" he said eagerly.

Just then, the nurse informed us that the doctor would be coming by shortly to finalize his discharge. Moments later, Robert's therapy team arrived, each one stopping in to say their goodbyes.

One by one, they encouraged Robert to keep pushing forward, reminding him that he would regain his full strength with time. They urged him to prioritize his health, to stay committed to his therapy, and to keep believing in his recovery. Some shook his hand, while others gave him a warm embrace.

A little while later, my phone rang—it was Pastor DeeKee.

"What time are you all heading out?" he asked.

"Soon!" I replied.

"I'm on my way," he said.

While waiting, I began packing up Robert's belongings, making sure everything was in order. Then, I helped him into the bathroom to change. His steps were slow, but he was standing. That alone was a reason to be thankful.

A knock at the door signaled Pastor DeeKee's arrival.

Robert stepped out of the bathroom, and a broad smile spread across Pastor DeeKee's face. "Man, you look good!"

They exchanged greetings before Pastor DeeKee turned to me. "Sis, you are a blessing," he said. "You have been with this man every single day. From morning until night, you've never left his side. Robert, you are a blessed man."

Robert nodded, "I know."

Soon, Dr. Neckritz arrived with Robert's discharge papers in hand. "Everything is in order," he said, "You're free to go!"

With that, we were officially heading home.

The Journey Home

Pastor DeeKee helped carry Robert's bag while the nurses assisted in getting him into a wheelchair. As we moved toward the exit, we passed by the nutrition staff in the hallway.

"Would it be possible to take a few of the meal menus with us?" I asked one of the staff members.

"Of course!" she said, handing me a few, "These will give you good meal ideas for Robert's recovery."

"Thank you!" I said, tucking them into my bag.

As we reached the hospital entrance, I left Robert and Pastor DeeKee at the curb while I went to get the car. Once I pulled up, I carefully helped Robert inside.

"Where to first?" I asked.

Without hesitation, Robert answered, "The barber shop."

I smiled, "Let's go!"

After getting him a fresh haircut, we stopped by the pharmacy to pick up his prescriptions and then made a quick trip to the grocery store to buy everything he would need.

Finally, we arrived home.

As Robert stepped inside, he grew quiet, taking in his surroundings. He didn't say a word, but I could feel the weight of the moment.

The Monnity Miracle

If he had spoken, I knew what he would have said:

"Thank You, Lord, for bringing me home."

I quickly prepared lunch for him and then began logging his blood pressure in a new daily record. I had purchased a blood pressure monitor from Amazon, determined to track every detail of his health. His prescriptions were neatly arranged on the table, and I had even invested in a serving tray—just in case he was too weak to sit at the table for meals.

I had thought of everything.

I even bought a treadmill for us.

I scheduled six weeks of inpatient and outpatient therapy. Every detail had been carefully planned. My priority was ensuring Robert's full recovery—and doing so in peace.

As I looked over at him, sitting comfortably in his own home, I knew in my heart—he was going to be okay.

And I was right.

Robert made a full recovery.

Not only did he regain his strength, but he also returned to work.

One of the first things we did after he got stronger was return to the music store where it all began. We wanted to personally thank everyone who played a role in saving his life that day.

As we stood there, I felt a wave of gratitude wash over me.

The Monnity Miracle

"From the bottom of my heart," I said, "thank you."

Tears filled my eyes as I realized just how much had been restored.

God had given us a second chance.

And we would never take it for granted.

God's Promise

Perseverance is the pathway to a new start because a new beginning often requires patience.

James 5:11

Each day, we ought to appreciate the opportunity for a fresh start; with patience, we can achieve anything.

Gallery

When we met.

Wedding day.

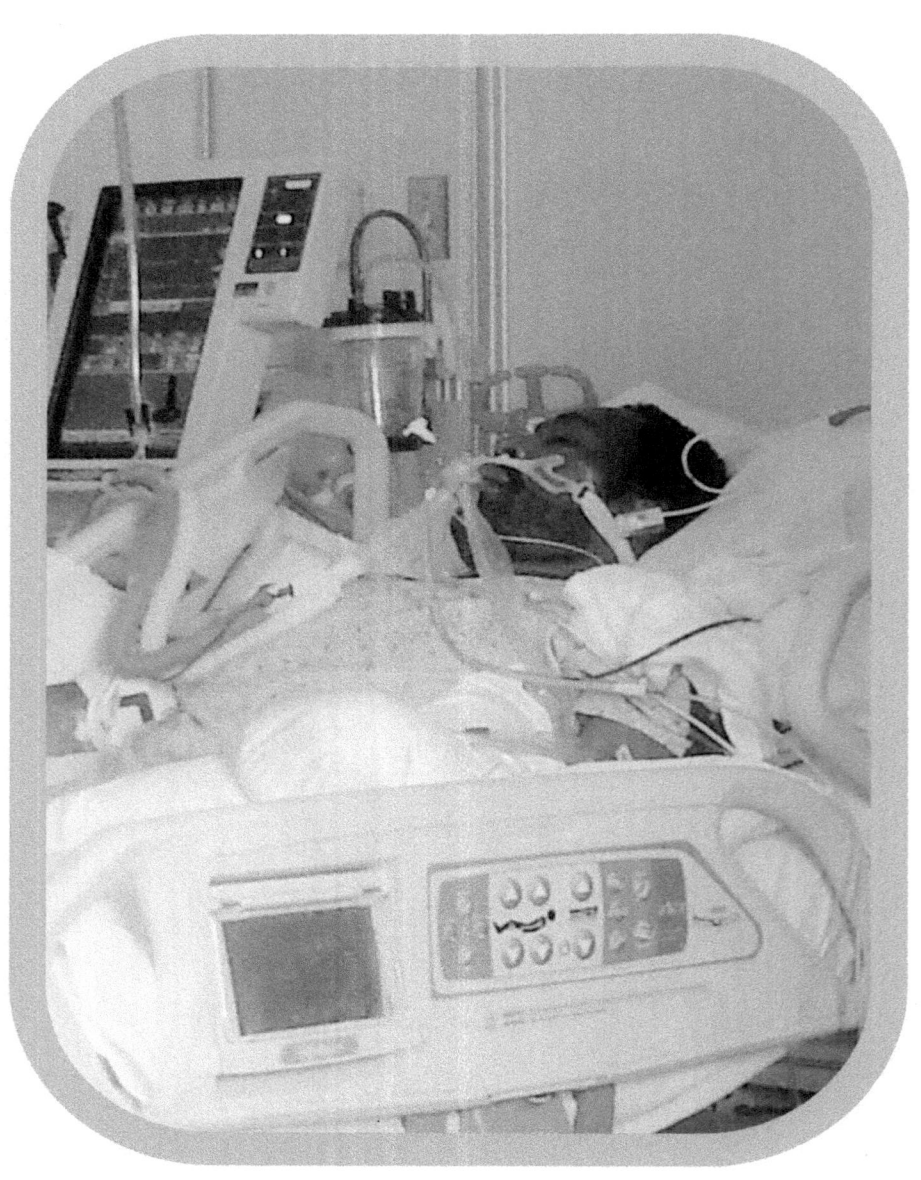

First time I saw him after the stroke.

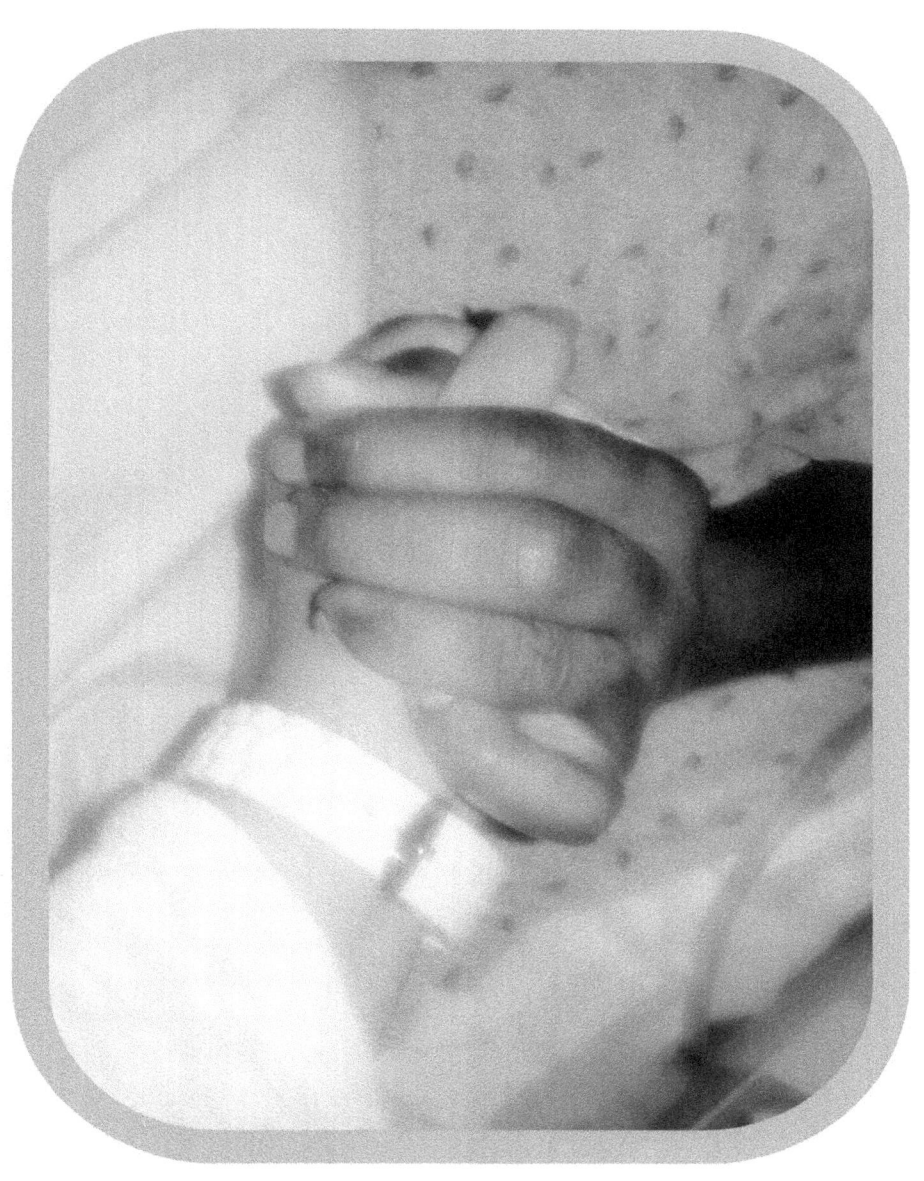

Holding his hand for prayer.

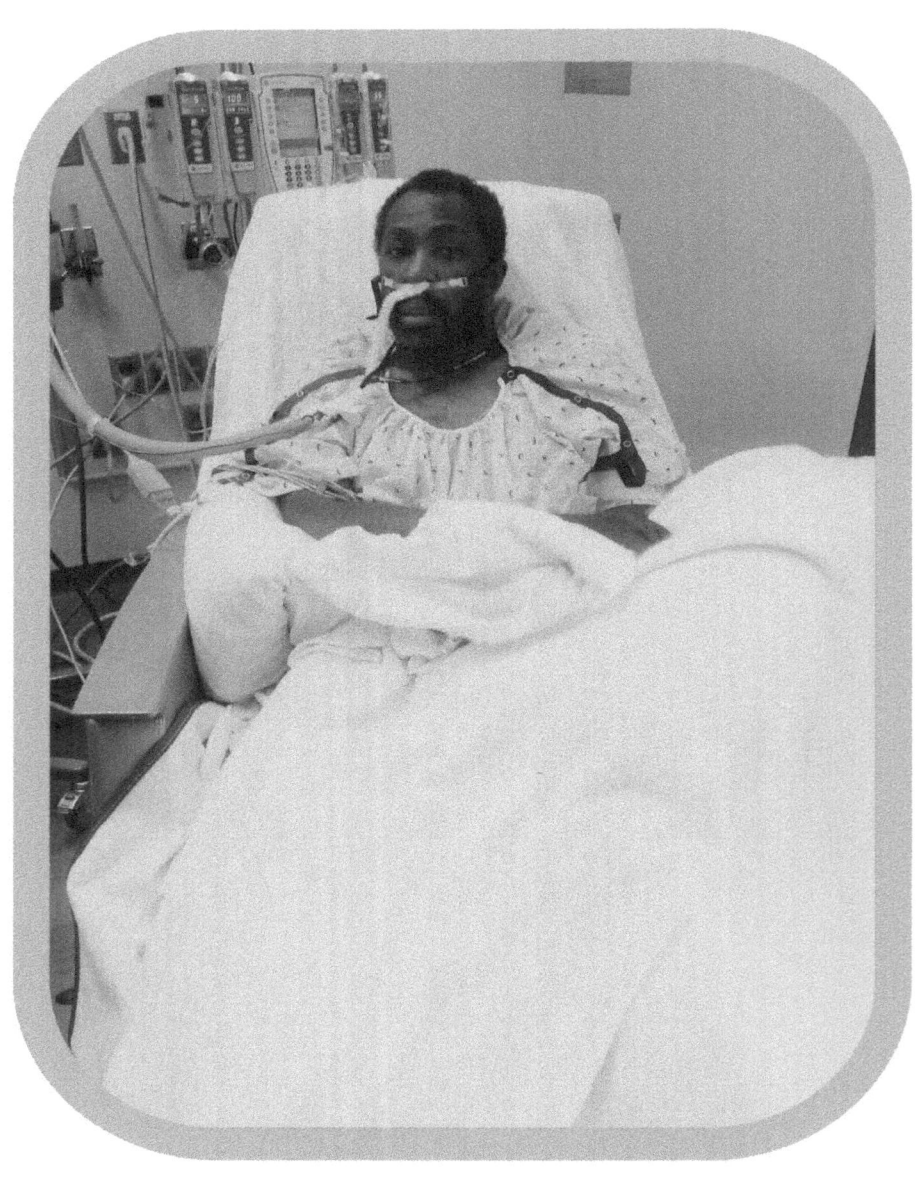

Taken off the ventilator
and sitting up for the first time.

Received good news.
His oxygen mask is coming off.

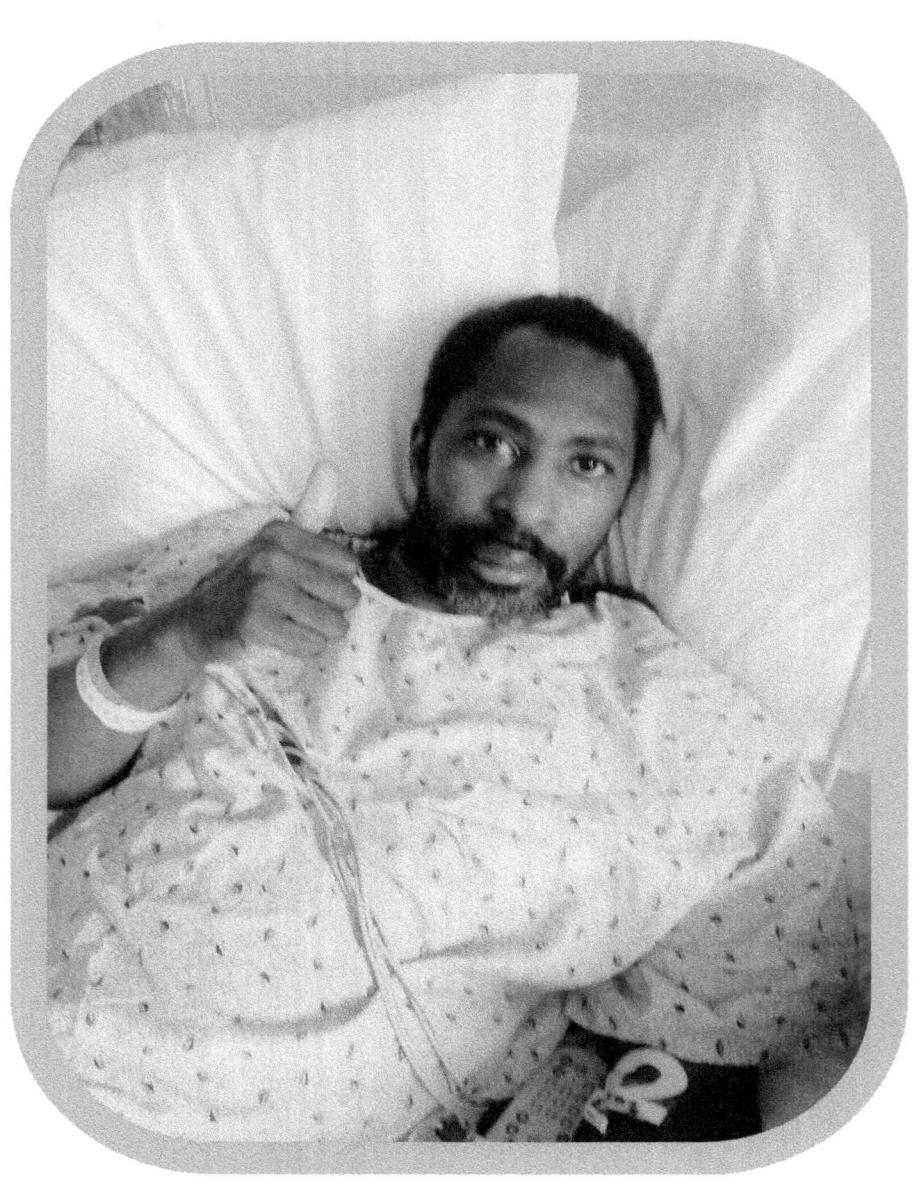

Oxygen mask was removed.

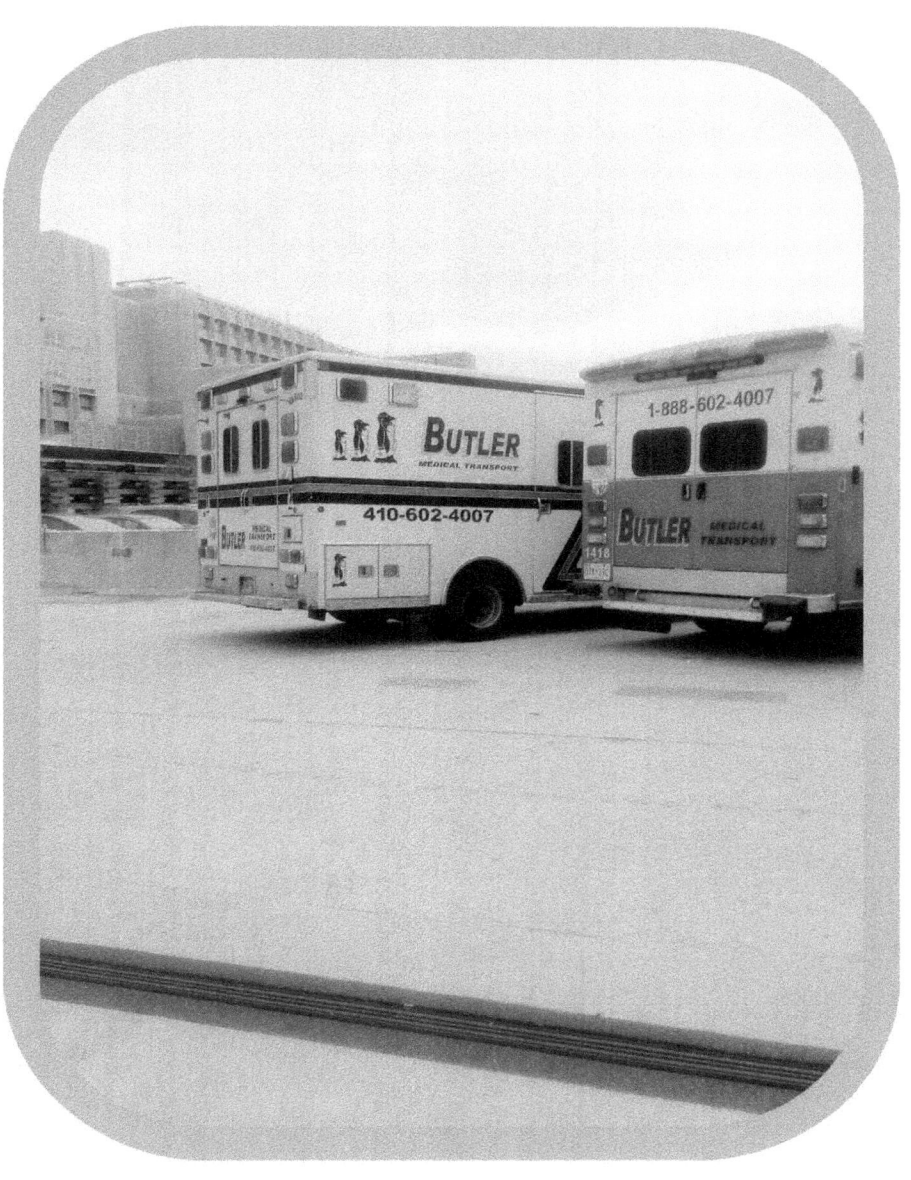

Butler transported us to
the rehab hospital.

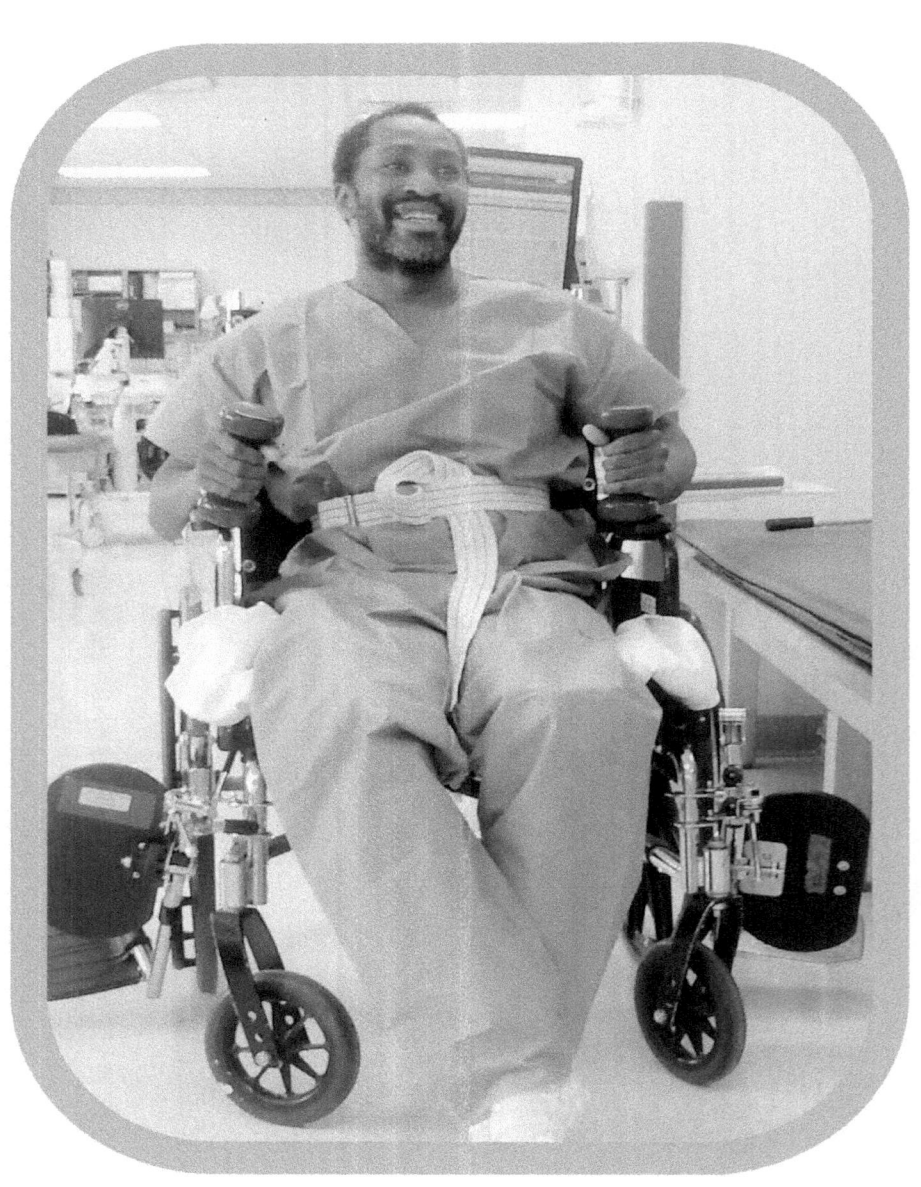

First day of occupational therapy.

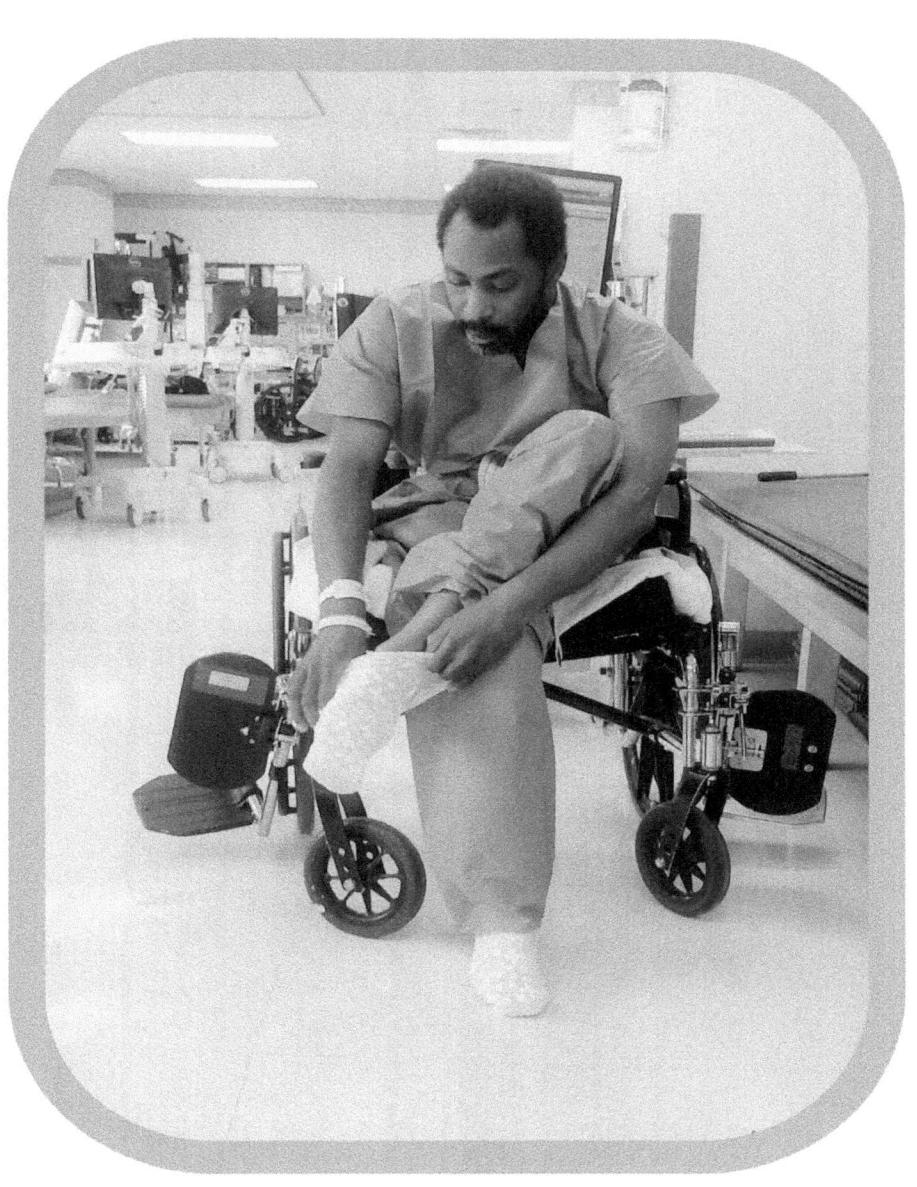

First day of occupational therapy.

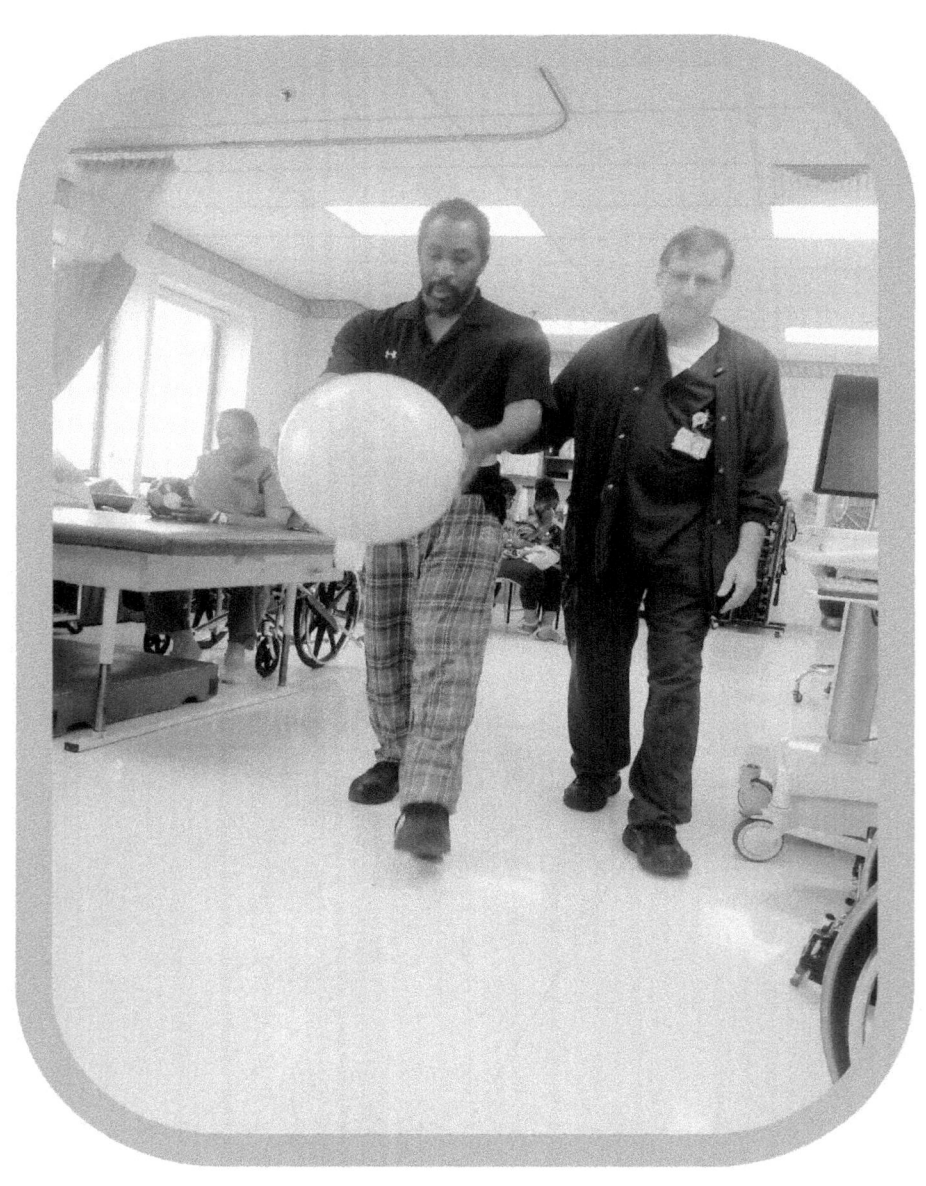

Second day of occupational therapy.

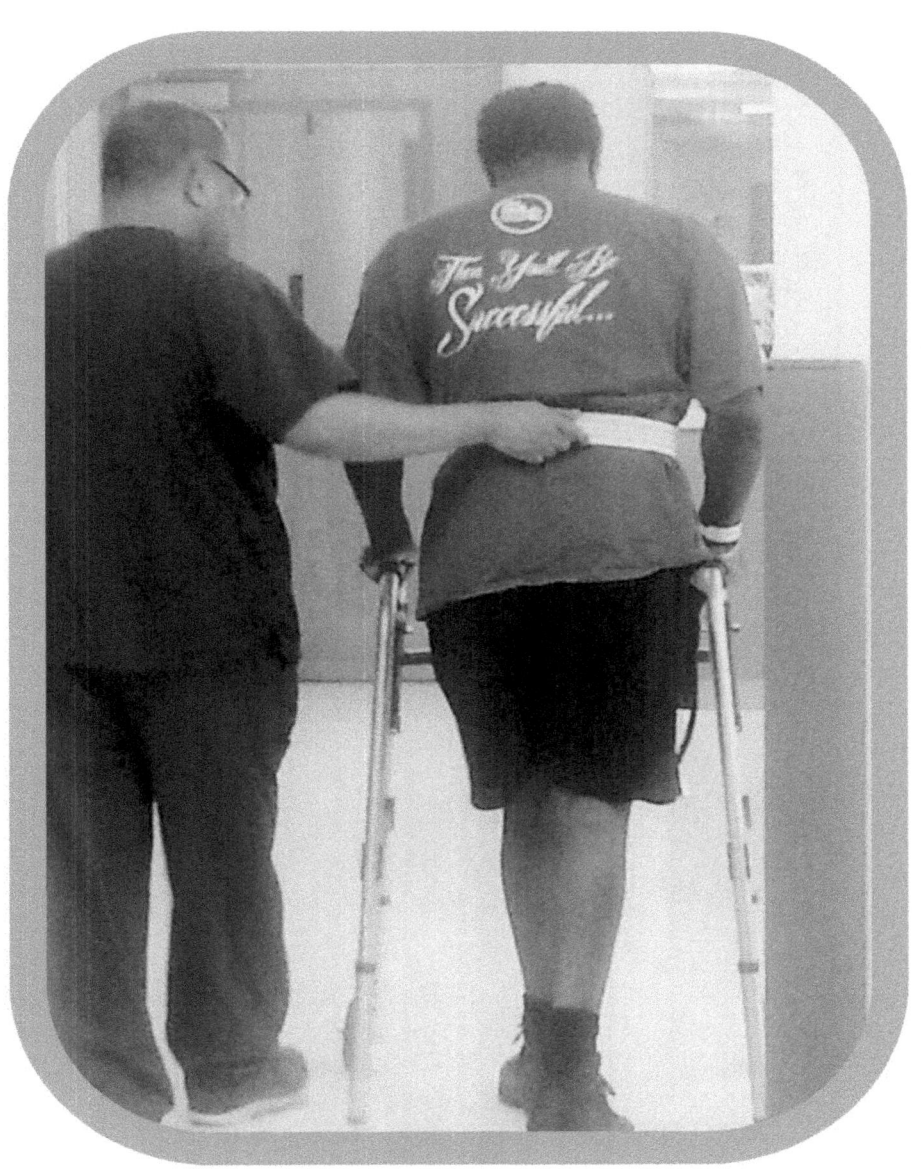

Third day of occupational therapy.

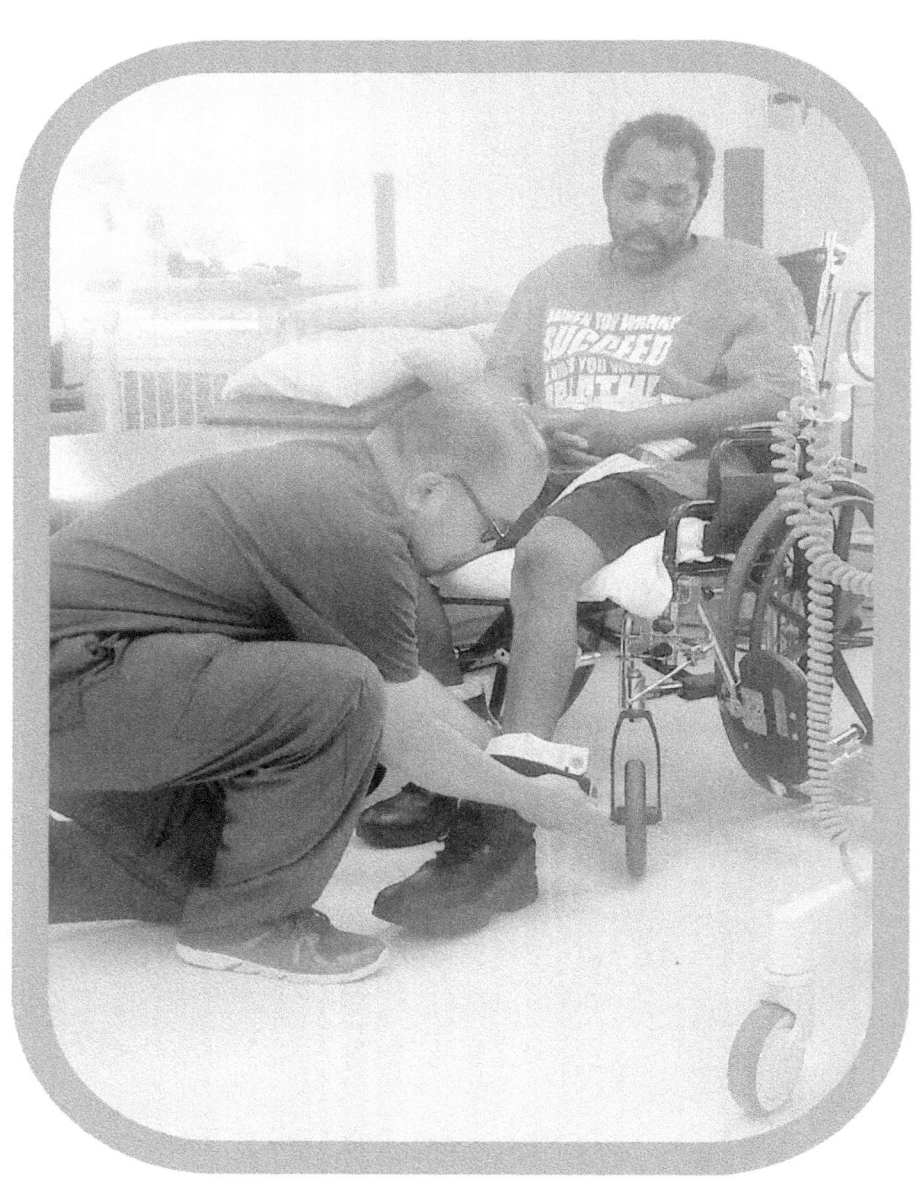

Third day of occupational therapy.

Third day of occupational therapy.

Third day of occupational therapy.

Third day of occupational therapy.

Third day of occupational therapy.

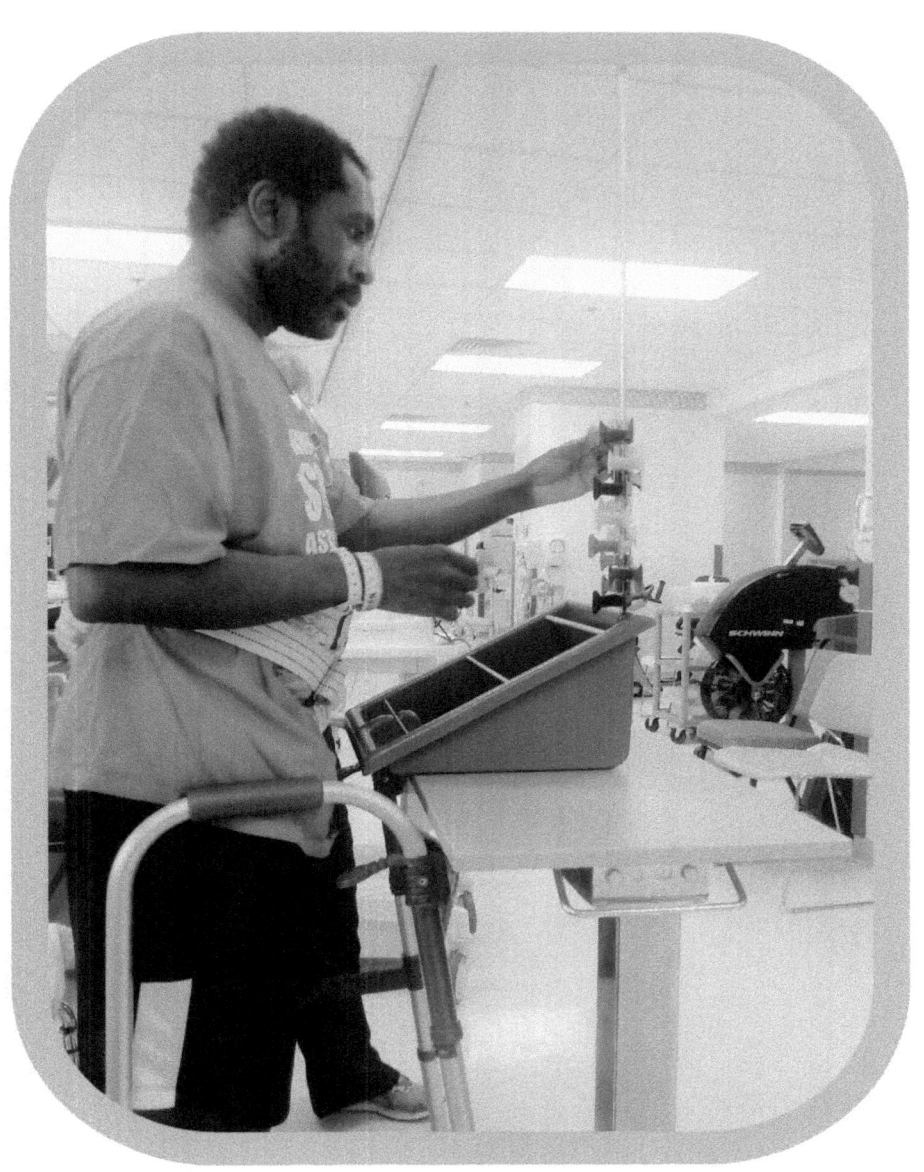

Third day of occupational therapy.

Third day of physical therapy.

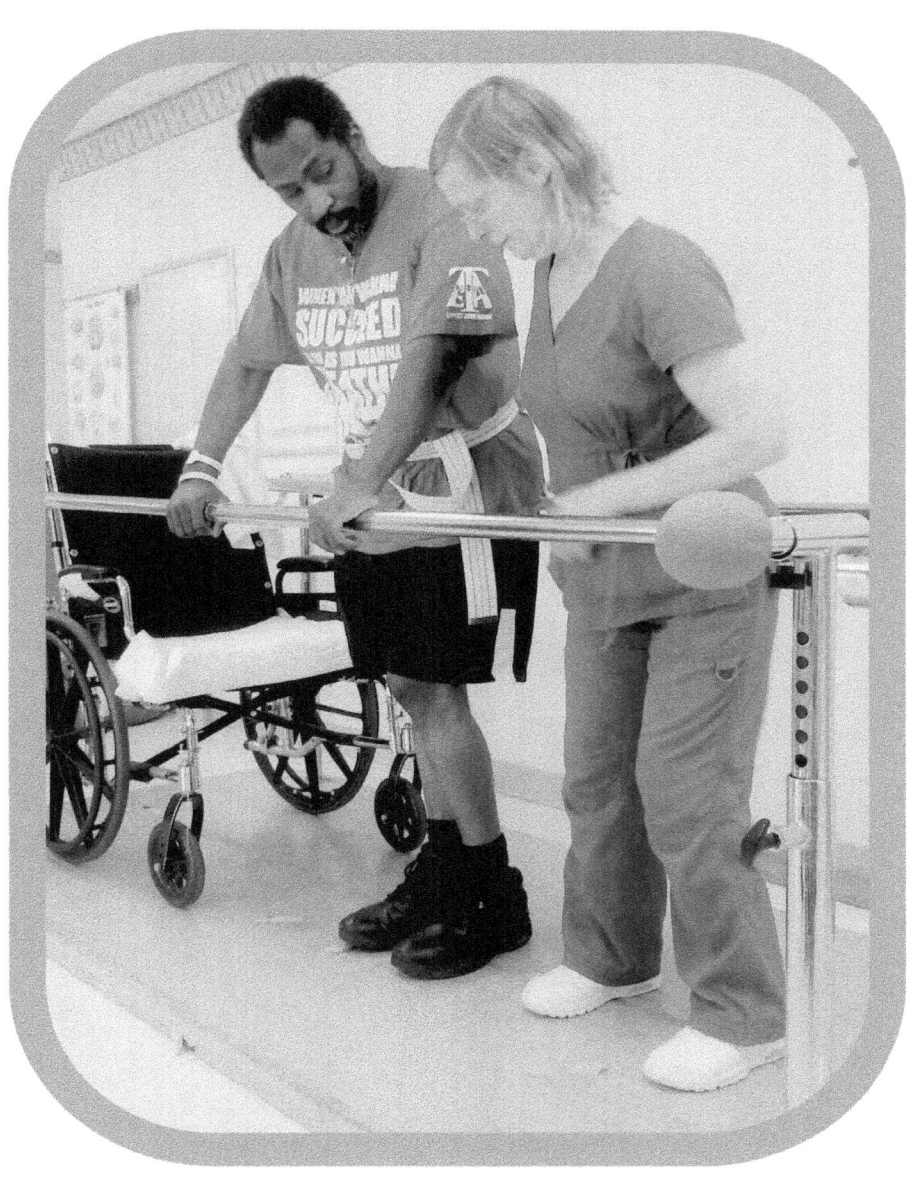

Third day of physical therapy.

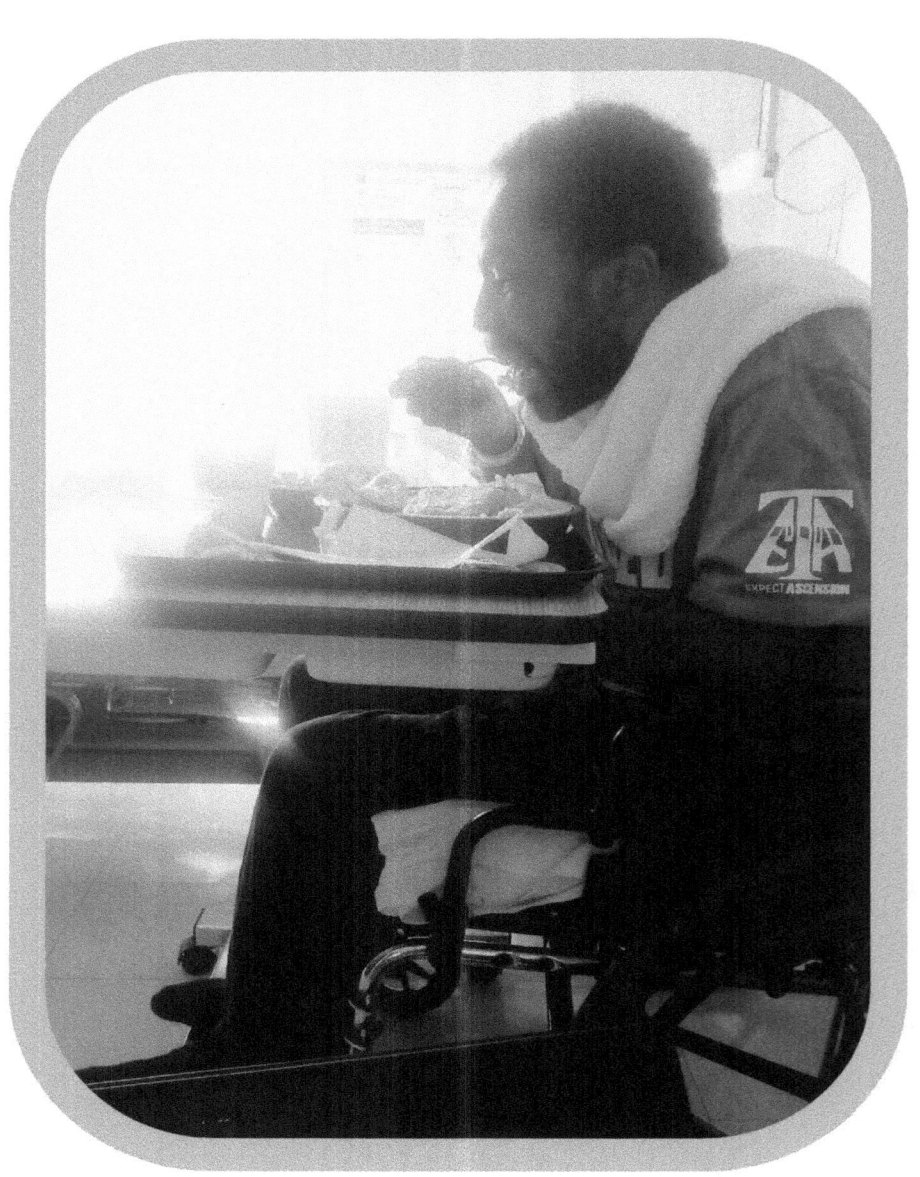

Eating lunch after morning therapy.

Early in the morning before therapy.

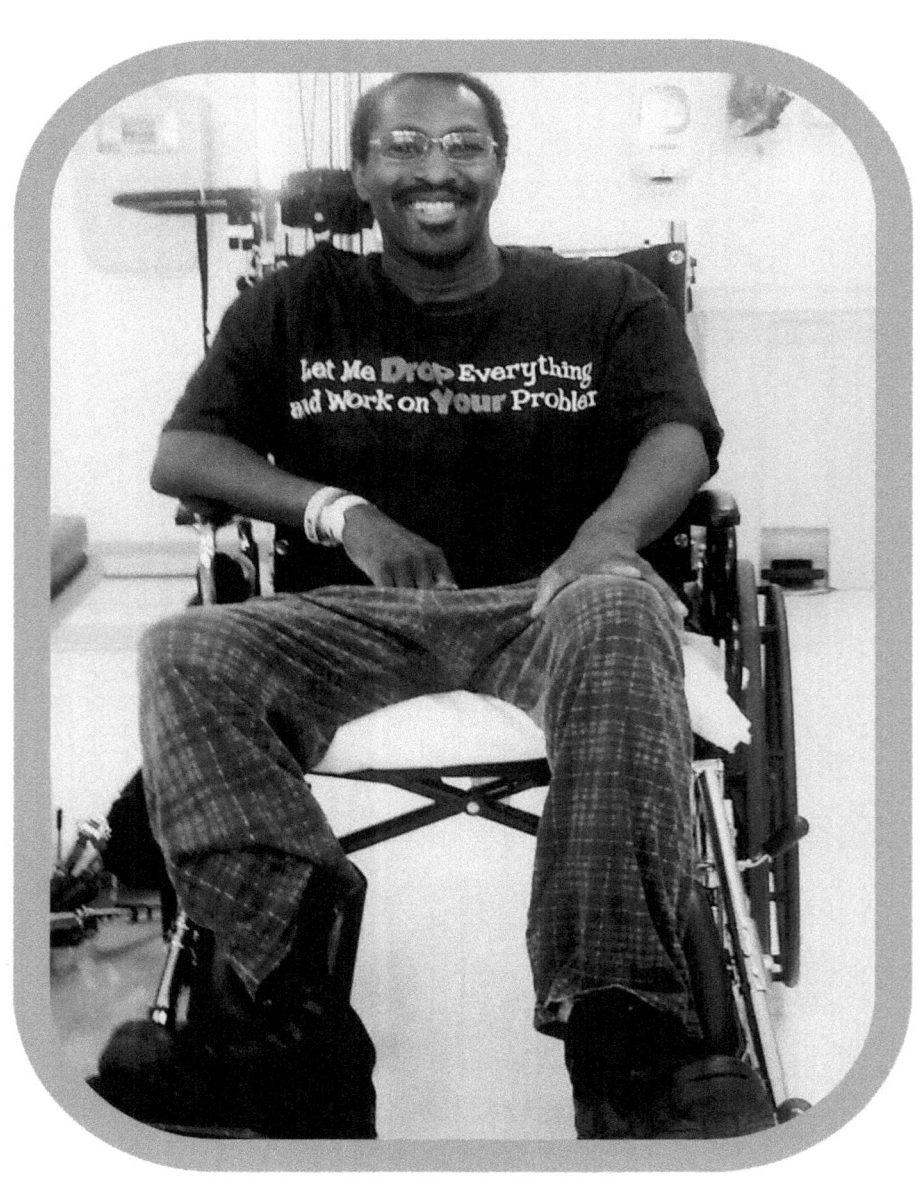

Fourth day. Preparing for
occupational therapy in the morning.

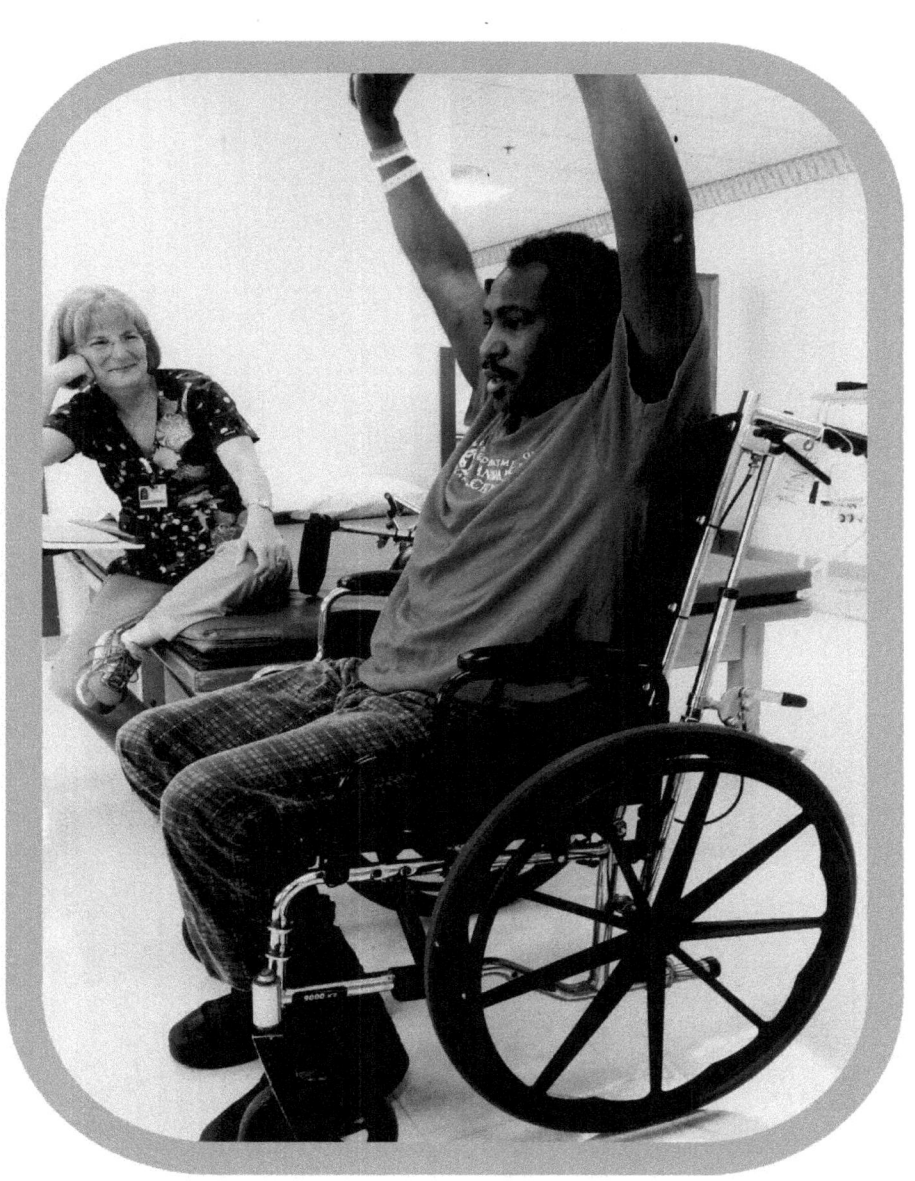

Fourth day of occupational therapy
in the afternoon.

Back in his room after morning
therapy playing Uno.

Falling asleep after playing Uno.

First time he stood on his own
outside in the gazebo.

Us celebrating him standing
for the first time.

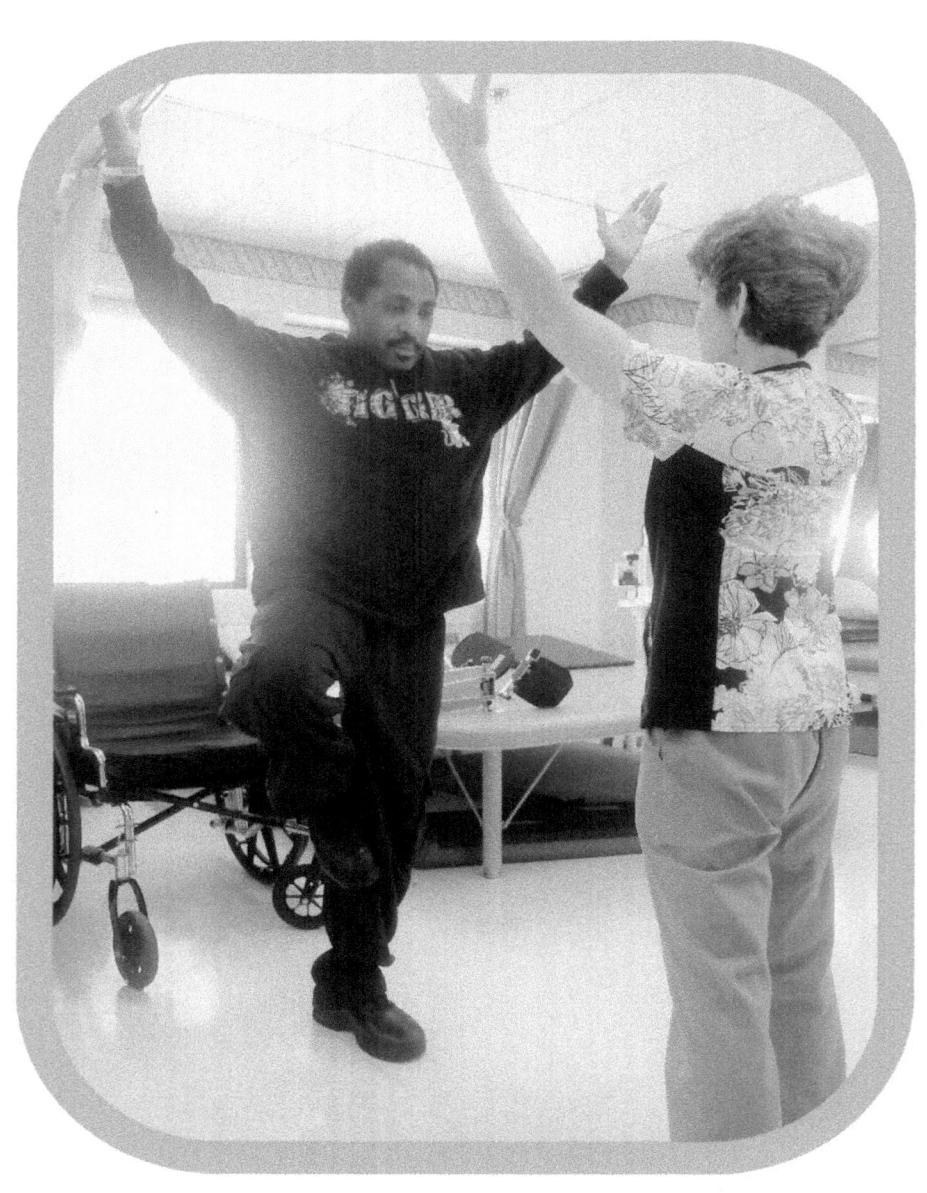

Final day of physical therapy.

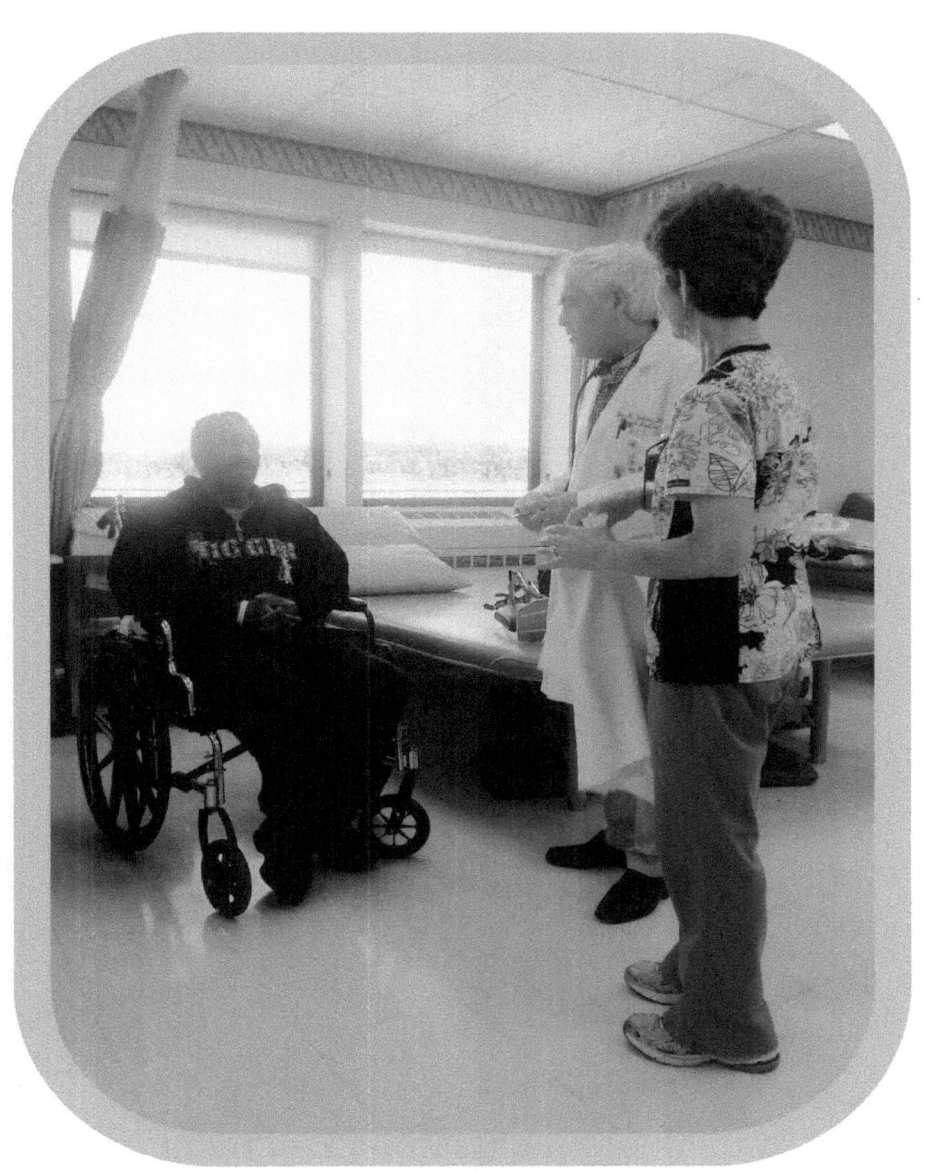

Dr. Neckritz tells us he can go home
and gives him final instructions.

We have been given the news
that we can go home. So happy.

Pastor DeeKee comes to visit before
we were released from the rehab hospital.

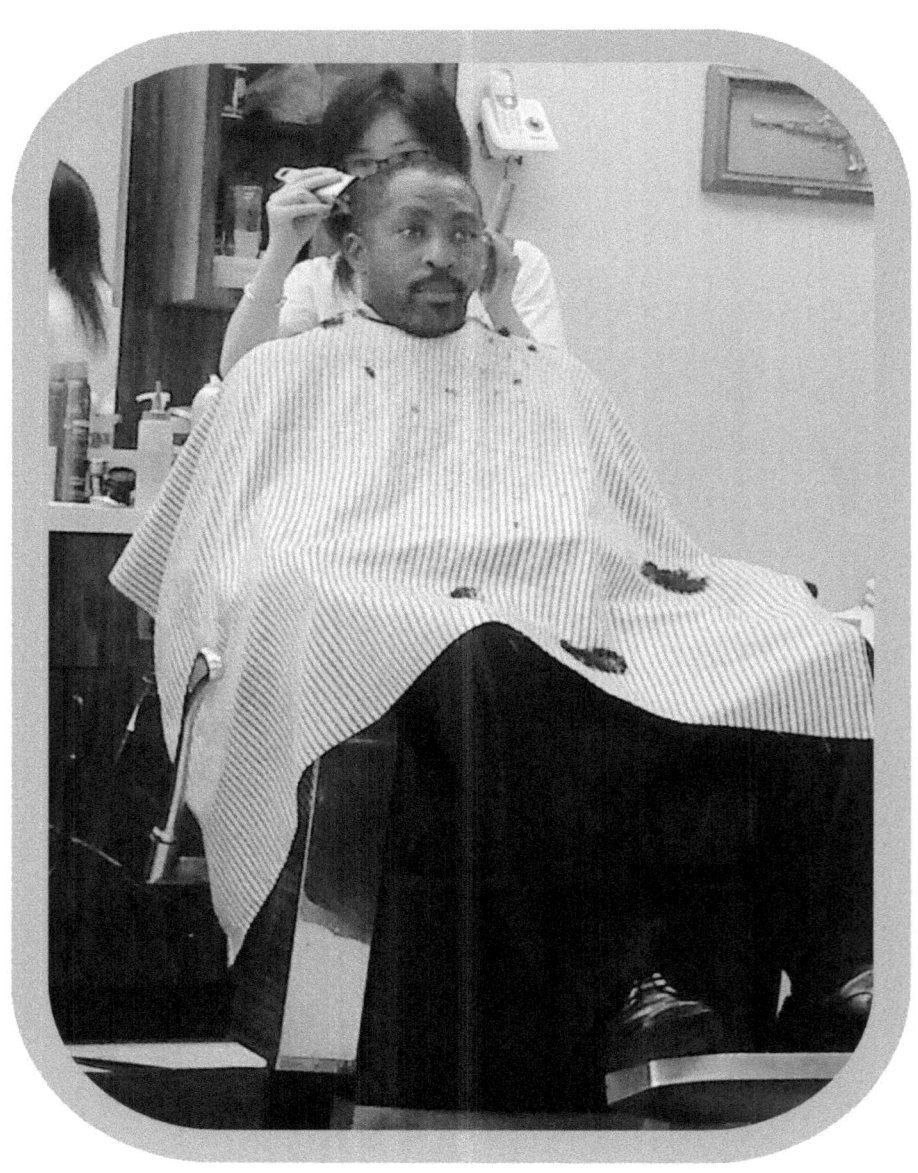

The barber shop.

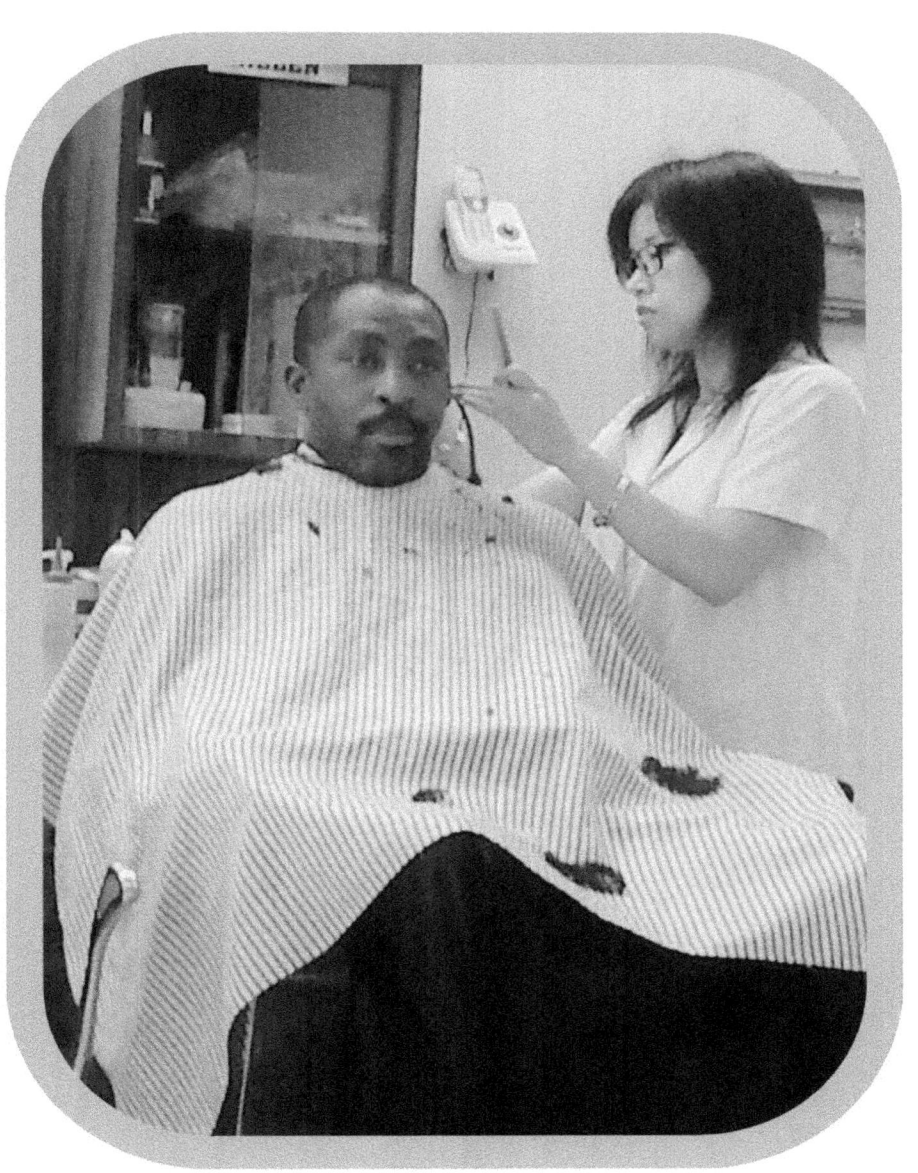

The barber shop.

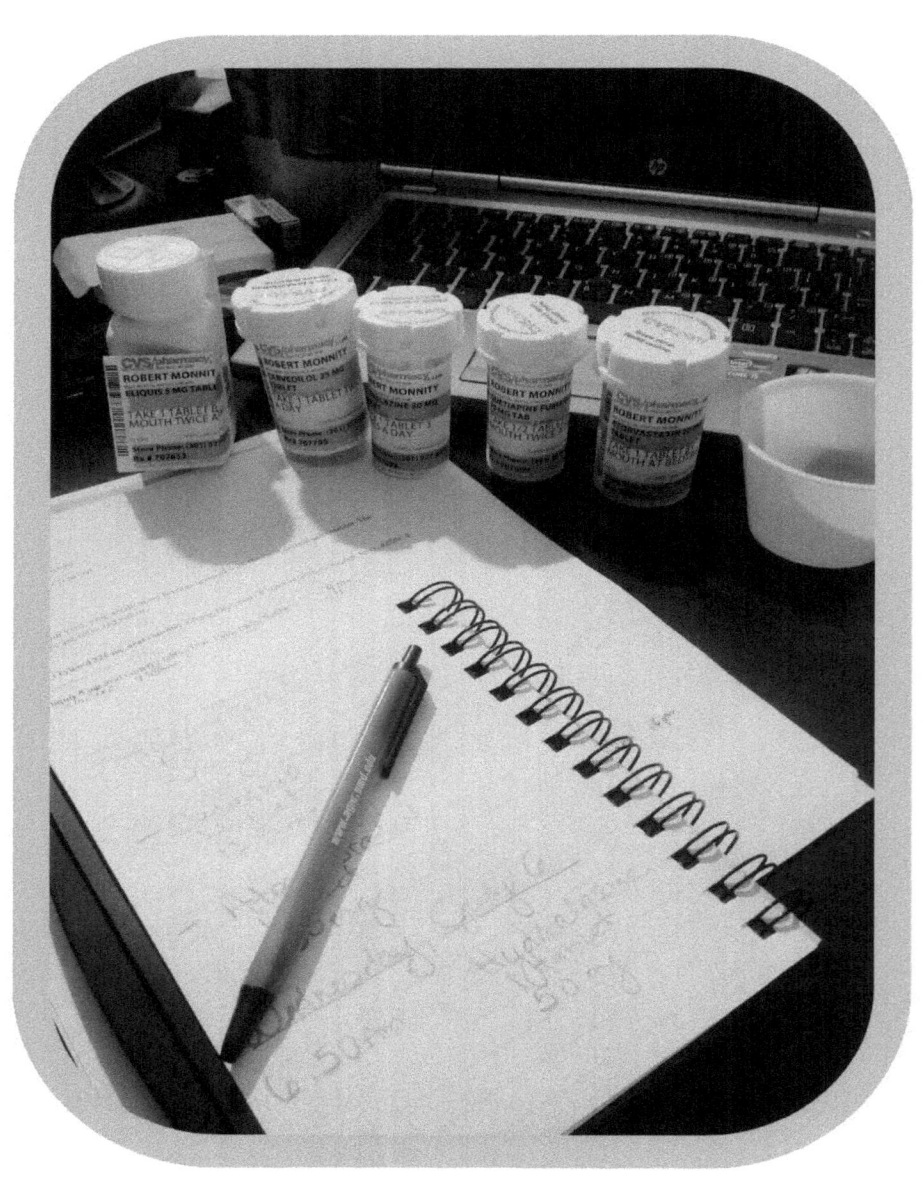

Started Medication Journal.

Breakfast

Lunch

Dinner

Breakfast

Lunch

Dinner

Breakfast

Lunch

Dinner

Breakfast

Lunch

Dinner

Us returning to the music store
where it started.

Recovering at home.

Celebrating his 46th birthday.

About the Author

Dr. Tyra C. Monnity, hailing from Hyattsville, Maryland, is a dynamic author, visionary entrepreneur, dedicated mentor, motivational speaker, and compassionate life coach. Rooted in her strong Christian faith, Dr. Monnity is passionate about uplifting and empowering others to navigate life's challenges with resilience and unwavering belief. She encourages individuals to find hope and take action during life's most critical moments, inspiring them to stand as advocates for their loved ones when they cannot advocate for themselves. Dr. Monnity's mission is to remind the world that miracles are possible through faith, love, and proactive support.

www.ingramcontent.com/pod-product-compliance
Lightning Source LLC
Chambersburg PA
CBHW041627140626
46547CB00031B/1155